Illegal
IMMIGRATION

OPPOSING
VIEWPOINTS®

Other Books of Related Interest

Illegal
IMMIGRATION

OPPOSING
VIEWPOINTS®

William Dudley, *Book Editor*

Daniel Leone, *President*
Bonnie Szumski, *Publisher*
Scott Barbour, *Managing Editor*

OPPOSING
VIEWPOINTS®
SERIES

GREENHAVEN PRESS
SAN DIEGO, CALIFORNIA

GALE GROUP
THOMSON LEARNING
Detroit • New York • San Diego • San Francisco
Boston • New Haven, Conn. • Waterville, Maine
London • Munich

Cover photo: Photodisc

Library of Congress Cataloging-in-Publication Data

Illegal immigration : opposing viewpoints / William Dudley, book
editor.
    p. cm. — (Opposing viewpoints series)
    Includes bibliographical references and index.
    ISBN 0-7377-0910-3 (pbk. : alk. paper) —
  ISBN 0-7377-0911-1 (lib. : alk. paper)
    1. Illegal aliens—Government policy—United States.
2. Illegal aliens—United States. I. Dudley, William, 1964–
II. Opposing viewpoints series (Unnumbered)

JV6483 .I54 2002
325.73—dc21   2001040733

Copyright © 2002 by Greenhaven Press,
an imprint of The Gale Group
10911 Technology Place, San Diego, CA 92127

"Congress shall make
no law...abridging the
freedom of speech, or of
the press."

First Amendment to the U.S. Constitution

The basic foundation of our democracy is the First
Amendment guarantee of freedom of expression.
The Opposing Viewpoints Series is dedicated to the
concept of this basic freedom and the idea that it is
more important to practice it than to enshrine it.

Contents

Why Consider Opposing Viewpoints?

"The only way in which a human being can make some approach to knowing the whole of a subject is by hearing what can be said about it by persons of every variety of opinion and studying all modes in which it can be looked at by every character of mind. No wise man ever acquired his wisdom in any mode but this."

John Stuart Mill

In our media-intensive culture it is not difficult to find differing opinions. Thousands of newspapers and magazines and dozens of radio and television talk shows resound with differing points of view. The difficulty lies in deciding which opinion to agree with and which "experts" seem the most credible. The more inundated we become with differing opinions and claims, the more essential it is to hone critical reading and thinking skills to evaluate these ideas. Opposing Viewpoints books address this problem directly by presenting stimulating debates that can be used to enhance and teach these skills. The varied opinions contained in each book examine many different aspects of a single issue. While examining these conveniently edited opposing views, readers can develop critical thinking skills such as the ability to compare and contrast authors' credibility, facts, argumentation styles, use of persuasive techniques, and other stylistic tools. In short, the Opposing Viewpoints Series is an ideal way to attain the higher-level thinking and reading skills so essential in a culture of diverse and contradictory opinions.

In addition to providing a tool for critical thinking, Opposing Viewpoints books challenge readers to question their own strongly held opinions and assumptions. Most people form their opinions on the basis of upbringing, peer pressure, and personal, cultural, or professional bias. By reading carefully balanced opposing views, readers must directly confront new ideas as well as the opinions of those with whom they disagree. This is not to simplistically argue that everyone who reads opposing views will—or should—change his or her opinion. Instead, the series enhances readers' understanding of their own views by encouraging confrontation with opposing ideas. Careful examination of others' views can lead to the readers' understanding of the logical inconsistencies in their own opinions, perspective on why they hold an opinion, and the consideration of the possibility that their opinion requires further evaluation.

Evaluating Other Opinions

To ensure that this type of examination occurs, Opposing Viewpoints books present all types of opinions. Prominent spokespeople on different sides of each issue as well as well-known professionals from many disciplines challenge the reader. An additional goal of the series is to provide a forum for other, less known, or even unpopular viewpoints. The opinion of an ordinary person who has had to make the decision to cut off life support from a terminally ill relative, for example, may be just as valuable and provide just as much insight as a medical ethicist's professional opinion. The editors have two additional purposes in including these less known views. One, the editors encourage readers to respect others' opinions—even when not enhanced by professional credibility. It is only by reading or listening to and objectively evaluating others' ideas that one can determine whether they are worthy of consideration. Two, the inclusion of such viewpoints encourages the important critical thinking skill of objectively evaluating an author's credentials and bias. This evaluation will illuminate an author's reasons for taking a particular stance on an issue and will aid in readers' evaluation of the author's ideas.

It is our hope that these books will give readers a deeper understanding of the issues debated and an appreciation of the complexity of even seemingly simple issues when good and honest people disagree. This awareness is particularly important in a democratic society such as ours in which people enter into public debate to determine the common good. Those with whom one disagrees should not be regarded as enemies but rather as people whose views deserve careful examination and may shed light on one's own.

Thomas Jefferson once said that "difference of opinion leads to inquiry, and inquiry to truth." Jefferson, a broadly educated man, argued that "if a nation expects to be ignorant and free . . . it expects what never was and never will be." As individuals and as a nation, it is imperative that we consider the opinions of others and examine them with skill and discernment. The Opposing Viewpoints Series is intended to help readers achieve this goal.

David L. Bender and Bruno Leone,
Founders

Greenhaven Press anthologies primarily consist of previously published material taken from a variety of sources, including periodicals, books, scholarly journals, newspapers, government documents, and position papers from private and public organizations. These original sources are often edited for length and to ensure their accessibility for a young adult audience. The anthology editors also change the original titles of these works in order to clearly present the main thesis of each viewpoint and to explicitly indicate the opinion presented in the viewpoint. These alterations are made in consideration of both the reading and comprehension levels of a young adult audience. Every effort is made to ensure that Greenhaven Press accurately reflects the original intent of the authors included in this anthology.

Introduction

"We are truly a nation of immigrants. But we are also a nation of laws."

—Brent Ashabranner

Rafael Vega, an Illinois resident featured in a *Chicago Tribune* article, is a hard worker who drives to several factory jobs. He wants to obtain a driver's license, but is unable to because he cannot provide a Social Security number on the application. Vega is an illegal immigrant, one of an estimated 300,000 in the state of Illinois.

Vega's dilemma is an example of how illegal immigrants face predicaments about items most Americans take for granted, but it also reveals a societal divide over how immigrants should be treated. Some states, such as North Carolina and Utah, have made illegal immigrants eligible for driver's licenses. Proponents of this policy argue that it makes the roads safer for everyone by ensuring that all drivers pass tests and have insurance. Opponents counter that such a policy enables illegal immigrants to fraudulently obtain welfare benefits or to vote, and that it effectively legitimizes the criminal act of illegal immigration. The debate over licensing "shows the split over how to treat illegal immigrants" notes the *Chicago Tribune.* "Policymakers acknowledge their presence but remain torn over whether to treat them as criminals or as *de facto* members of society."

The presence of illegal immigrants in the United States is a product of the gap between the number of people allowed to legally immigrate to the United States and the global demand for U.S. residency. Every year hundreds of thousands of people from around the world attempt to enter and live in the United States. According to statistics kept by the Immigration and Naturalization Service (INS), from 1992 to 1998 825,000 people on average annually immigrated and became legal permanent residents of the United States. Some of them were issued immigrant visas at U.S. consulates abroad; others were temporary U.S. residents who successfully petitioned the government to adjust their status from temporary to permanent.

Obtaining an immigrant visa can be a drawn-out endeavor. United States immigration law contains a complex array of preferences. Favored treatment is given to people who are closely related to a U.S. citizen or legal permanent resident, who are sponsored by an employer or have needed job skills, or who qualify as political refugees. Even for people who qualify within these categories, the wait before an immigrant visa is issued can last ten or fifteen years. The long waiting periods for immigrant visas is a stark reminder of the fact that the United States, despite its reputation as a "nation of immigrants," does not have an open border policy. America admits more legal immigrants than most other nations, but still sets limits as to who and how many may come.

Despite government efforts to regulate immigration, the United States population includes millions of illegal immigrants who choose to ignore the law and become U.S. residents without official permission. Most come for reasons similar to those motivating legal immigrants—the desire for a better life, a better job, reunifying with relatives, or escaping oppressive conditions at home. Some sneak into the United States from Mexico or Canada without proper documentation. In 1996 alone the Border Patrol made 1.6 million apprehensions of people trying to enter the United States; most arrests occurred along the 1,952 mile U.S./ Mexico border. Other illegal immigrants receive permission to enter the United States on a temporary basis, as tourists or students for example, but then stay beyond the terms of their visas. These account for more than half of illegal immigrants in the United States. Still others may have lost their legal resident status after being convicted of a crime. The INS has estimated that five million illegal immigrants live in the United States. Other estimates, based on 2000 census data, have gone as high as eleven million. This was after Congress in 1986 attempted to "wipe the slate clean" by granting amnesty to most of America's illegal immigrant population at that time.

Critics of illegal immigration describe the presence of this number of illegal immigrants as an "invasion" that threatens the economic and social future of the United States. "The sovereignty of our nation is at risk from a flood of illegal im-

13

migrants who are usurping the benefits of being American citizens," writes columnist Ken Hamblin. Hamblin and others argue that the United States has limited resources and abilities to assimilate new immigrants, and that greater efforts should be made to prevent people from entering illegally, deport illegal immigrants who are found here, and punish employers of illegal immigrants. "Cruel as it may seem," Hamblin argues, "we cannot afford compassion" because that would only encourage more illegal immigration.

However, efforts to deport or otherwise punish or deter illegal immigrants often strike people as too harsh and inhumane. Some people have questioned whether immigration prevention is the real motive behind immigration laws. Lisa Brodyaga, a lawyer for a refugee shelter in Harlingen, Texas and immigrant rights advocate, has criticized recent federal statutes including one requiring illegal immigrants to return to their country of origin and wait ten years before applying for a legal immigrant visa. "Do they [members of Congress] really believe that a person who has grown up here will leave the U.S. and wait 10 years to come back? Do they really believe that these new . . . laws will result in their stated goals [of] keeping people out who have been here illegally?" Brodyaga argues that these actions of Congress instead will create "an almost slave labor force—people who are undocumented, who are living here, and who can never claim their rights." Efforts should instead be made to include and treat illegal immigrants as full members of American society, Brodyaga and others argue, rather than try to exclude them or drive them away.

The question of whether to treat illegal immigrants as criminals, as victims, or as potential U.S. citizens lies at the heart of many of the debates about illegal immigration. *Illegal Immigration: Opposing Viewpoints* examines several of these questions in the following chapters: Do Illegal Immigrants Harm America? Are Illegal Immigrants Being Victimized? How Should America Respond to Immigration? Should U.S. Immigration and Refugee Policies Be Changed? The book's contributors provide a sampling of the sharp divisions of opinion that exist within this country over this important and controversial phenomenon of American life.

CHAPTER 1

Do Illegal Immigrants Harm America?

Chapter Preface

In a 2001 study, university researchers attempted to come up with the total costs associated with illegal immigration incurred by U.S. counties that bordered Mexico. The researchers determined that border counties in California, Arizona, and Texas paid $108 million in court, law enforcement, and medical expenses on illegal immigrants. This money was partially reimbursed by a federal program that compensates local governments for incarcerating illegal immigrant criminals, but in 1999 these counties received only $12.4 million, or about one-eighth of their expenses. This shortfall has been criticized by local political leaders. "Counties . . . are subsidizing the federal [immigration] policies" claimed Pima County, Arizona supervisor Sharon Bronson.

The study is one of several that have attempted to ascertain the costs and benefits that illegal immigrants bring to the United States and to its taxpayers. Such studies are difficult because of the challenges of collecting data on a population that generally keeps its status hidden from government officials. The impact of illegal immigrants on the nation's tax bill is also hard to measure because illegal immigrants generate tax revenues as well as costs. Many pay Social Security taxes on their wages using falsely obtained numbers; the result is that they pay into the Social Security system without ever receiving benefits. Illegal immigrants also generate tax revenue by paying sales taxes when they buy goods. A 1996 study on Californian immigration by the Tomas Rivera Center, a Los Angles–based think tank, concluded that, contrary to costing money, each illegal immigrant in the long run produced an average net *profit* of almost eight thousand dollars for the state.

The impact on taxpayers is but one area in which critics say illegal immigrants harm the United States. Others include increased crime and the taking of jobs from American workers. The viewpoints in this chapter examine the validity of these and other concerns and fears about illegal immigrants and their effect on American society.

"Every day thousands of illegals stream across the 2,500 miles of border with Mexico."

Illegal Immigration Threatens America

Ted Hayes

Illegal immigration, especially from Mexico, threatens the United States in several different ways, according to the following viewpoint by Ted Hayes. He argues that illegal immigrants harm America's economy by using up social services and by taking jobs that otherwise would go to Americans. They harm American culture by refusing to assimilate within it and maintaining a foreign cultural identity. Finally, Hayes contends that they threaten America's sovereignty because the United States is losing control over who comes over its borders. A former instructor in political science at the University of California, Berkeley, Hayes currently resides in San Diego where he writes on politics and culture.

As you read, consider the following questions:

1. What is meant by "Aztlan" and how is it related to America's immigration problem, according to Hayes?
2. What forces and actors are frustrating the process of immigrant assimilation, in the author's view?
3. What actions has the United States taken in the past against illegal immigration, as stated by Hayes?

From "Illegal Immigration Threatens U.S. Sovereignty, Economy and Culture," by Ted Hayes, *Insight on the News*, September 25, 2000. Copyright © 2000 by Insight Magazine. Reprinted with permission.

E very day thousands of illegals stream across the 2,500 miles of border with Mexico. According to the U.S. Immigration and Naturalization Service, or INS, the total number of illegals in America from this source increases by 275,000 annually. Already the United States is host to an illegal population of 7 to 12 million, of whom the vast majority are Mexican or Hispanic in origin. These illegal and uninvited guests help themselves to jobs, education, welfare and unemployment compensation. The many whose wages are paid under the table pay little or no taxes. And they are easy prey for unscrupulous employers and politicians. What a new president and Congress decide to do about this when they take office in January 2001 matters a great deal.

Disturbing Signs

Despite the soothing reassurances of the liberal left—that America is a nation of immigrants, and illegal immigrants are just more of the same—all the signs suggest the opposite.

Item: Across the six states of the American Southwest are colleges and universities teaching Chicano studies, the core argument of which is that the Southwest was taken illegally by the United States during the Mexican-American War of 1846–48, and that these states should now secede from the Union to create a new, Mexican-based nation, "Aztlan." The most widely used text in these programs, Rodolfo Acuna's *Occupied America*, calls the Mexican-American War "as vicious as that of Hitler's invasion of Poland" and shows a map of Mexico stretching up as far as Kansas. Hundreds of thousands of American college students, including many young Mexican-Americans, have absorbed this political indoctrination.

Item: In a study conducted in 1994, then-governor of California Pete Wilson discovered that the cost of illegals to California, in unemployment, medical, educational and other services, was more than $4 billion annually. California's Proposition 187, which passed in the wake of this study, prohibited most public benefits to illegals, including education, but was overturned by the courts in 1998.

Item: In California and Arizona, thousands of illegal Mexicans work six months in one state while collecting unemployment in the other and then move to the second to col-

Illegal Aliens: Our Eighth Largest State?

Northeastern University estimates there are 11 million illegal immigrants in the United States. That is more than the population of 43 states and 6 Central American nations, and about 20 times the difference in the 2000 presidential election.

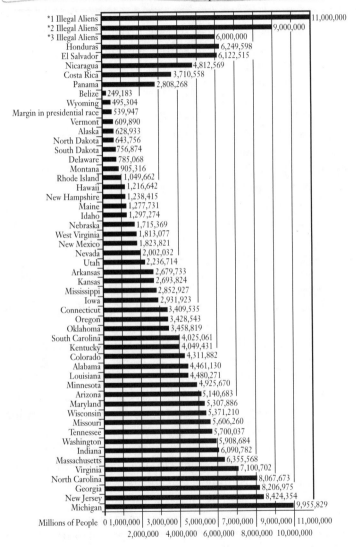

*1 Illegal Aliens	11,000,000
*2 Illegal Aliens	9,000,000
*3 Illegal Aliens	6,000,000
Honduras	6,249,598
El Salvador	6,122,515
Nicaragua	4,812,569
Costa Rica	3,710,558
Panama	2,808,268
Belize	249,183
Wyoming	495,304
Margin in presidential race	539,947
Vermont	609,890
Alaska	628,933
North Dakota	643,756
South Dakota	756,874
Delaware	785,068
Montana	905,316
Rhode Island	1,049,662
Hawaii	1,216,642
New Hampshire	1,238,415
Maine	1,277,731
Idaho	1,297,274
Nebraska	1,715,369
West Virginia	1,813,077
New Mexico	1,823,821
Nevada	2,002,032
Utah	2,236,714
Arkansas	2,679,733
Kansas	2,693,824
Mississippi	2,852,927
Iowa	2,931,923
Connecticut	3,409,535
Oregon	3,428,543
Oklahoma	3,458,819
South Carolina	4,025,061
Kentucky	4,049,431
Colorado	4,311,882
Alabama	4,461,130
Louisiana	4,480,271
Minnesota	4,925,670
Arizona	5,140,683
Maryland	5,307,886
Wisconsin	5,371,210
Missouri	5,606,260
Tennessee	5,700,037
Washington	5,908,684
Indiana	6,090,782
Massachusetts	6,355,568
Virginia	7,100,702
North Carolina	8,067,673
Georgia	8,206,975
New Jersey	8,424,354
Michigan	9,955,829

Millions of People 0 1,000,000 2,000,000 3,000,000 4,000,000 5,000,000 6,000,000 7,000,000 8,000,000 9,000,000 10,000,000 11,000,000

*1. Estimate by Northeastern University. *2. Adjusted Census Bureau estimate reported by the *Washington Post*. *3. Original Census Bureau estimate. Numbers for Central American nations are from the *2001 World Almanac*. Numbers for U.S. states are from the 2000 U.S. Census.

lect unemployment from the first.

Item: The U.S. Border Patrol is undermanned. In 1998, while supporters of the Patrol in Congress were calling for a fourfold increase, the White House budget proposed for fiscal 1999 contained no money at all for additional agents.

Item: Agua Prieta, Mexico, just across the Rio Grande from Douglas, Ariz., is the largest staging ground for illegal immigration into the United States anywhere on the border. From campgrounds spread along several miles, well over 1,000 illegals cross into the United States every night of the year.

Immigrants Not Assimilating

To compound matters many of the new immigrants are assimilating slowly or not at all. As demonstrated by Peter Brimelow in *Alien Nation* (1996), waves of new settlers in the 19th century were willing to learn English and become a part of America, while periods of 40 to 50 years intervened between each wave to allow assimilation. But these factors are not present for illegals from Mexico, frustrating the normal process of political assimilation.

That process is further frustrated by several powerful actors and groups:

- The government of Mexico. Mexicans illegally in the United States repatriate millions of dollars annually to Mexico, a real boost for the government. Vicente Fox, the newly elected president of Mexico, flagrantly campaigned for Mexican votes in Southern California among legal and illegal Mexicans and at his first press conference called for unrestricted labor migration into the United States;
- American businessmen and lobbies. A ganglion of diverse interests exists to defend illegal immigration at every turn. Environmentalists protest the building of a fence to keep illegals out. Businessmen and suburban home owners want a cheap labor supply that can't be unionized. In June 2000 a newspaper in northern San Diego County called for dismantling the Border Patrol's checkpoint on Interstate 15 because it delays suburbanites on their drive home; and
- The philosophers of multiculturalism. Without overtly

advocating legal or illegal immigration, multiculturalism supports all the aspects of sustained nonassimila-
tion. It views bilingual teaching, mass rallies flying
Mexican flags, and the demand for the return of lands to
La Raza, as cultural justice, not political mischief.

America Must Protect Itself

Do we have control of our border with Mexico? Clearly, no.
Should we clamp down? Obviously, yes. The United States
may have its own Quebec problem soon: a rapidly growing
minority, many of whom are present illegally in the country,
insistent on keeping their own cultural identity and supported by the liberal establishment.

In the 1950s President Dwight D. Eisenhower, faced with
large numbers of Mexicans crossing the Rio Grande illegally, sent troops to the Mexican border. In six months Operation Wetback ended the problem. Do we dare take any
kind of effective action again—or does the border, and with
it American sovereignty, already belong to Mexico?

"The real point is that there isn't any immigration crisis."

Illegal Immigration Does Not Threaten America

Richard Rayner

Richard Rayner, a California resident who himself immigrated from England, is a writer and novelist. In the following viewpoint, he profiles an illegal immigrant and her children and argues that people like them do not constitute a national crisis. Illegal immigration is controversial, he writes, because it touches on several emotional issues, including crime, welfare, and the future of America. However, Rayner holds that the United States can easily absorb and indeed benefit from the labor and other contributions of both legal and illegal immigrants.

As you read, consider the following questions:

1. How does Maria T. represent a nightmare scenario of immigration, according to Rayner?
2. How many illegal immigrants enter the United States annually, according to the author?
3. According to Rayner, what role does race play in the immigration debate?

M aria T. bites her nails. At 31, with five children, she's one of the 1.7 million immigrants now estimated to be living in California illegally. She speaks almost no English, even though she has been in America for more than eight years. In her clean and sparsely furnished living room, her kids—Gustavo (11), Mario (7), Maribel (6), Cesar (5) and Joan (4)—are in front of the TV, laughing first at "Home Improvement," then at "The Simpsons."

The refrigerator is almost empty; it contains only a gallon of milk, some Kool-Aid, a few tortillas. Her life is frugal, a devotion to the future of her children. Though there are three bedrooms in the apartment, all five sleep with her because she hates to let them out of her sight. Since she has no car and can rarely afford the bus, the family walks everywhere, Maria leading the way like Mother Goose with the kids behind toting Batman and Pocahontas backpacks. On a typical day she walks six miles, shuttling between her apartment and the local school in Van Nuys. . . .

For her, as for so many, the decision to make the journey to El Norte was the beginning of an epic. Gustavo was 3 at the time, Mario was 8 months, and she was 5 months pregnant with Maribel. Maria crossed the border with the help of a "coyote," a guide, but when she arrived in San Diego the woman who'd paid for her brothers' crossings didn't have any money this time. Maria was kept a slave in the coyote's house. He beat and raped her until, after three months, her brother raised $300, half the sum agreed for the crossing, and the coyote let her go.

She stayed with her brother in Los Angeles, the Pico-Union district, and it was here that Maribel was born. "I'd come out of labor and I was staring at the wall and I said to my sister-in-law, 'Look, she's there.' She said, 'Who?' I said, 'The Virgin Mary.' She said: 'There's nothing there. You're crazy.' But it was true all the same. For eight months the Virgin would appear to me. She made me strong.

"At first I had to beg for food. Sometimes I did day work for Latinos, for $10 a day. I'd take off into the city on the bus, not really knowing where I was going, and get off to beg on the streets. I'm ashamed of that."

Slowly, she clawed her way up. It is in so many ways a

23

classic immigrant's tale, although she has been the beneficiary not just of her own drive, but also of something equally important—welfare. She's here illegally, with fake ID, and she doesn't work. She receives $723 in cash and $226 in food stamps, and Section 8 takes care of more than two-thirds of her $1,000 rent (high, because landlords know illegals won't complain).

It's a myth, however, that anyone can come over the border and start milking the system. Only Medicaid and limited food benefits are available to illegal immigrants, and most don't apply for these because they fear detection by the Immigration and Naturalization Service (I.N.S.). Maria T. gets what she does because of those of her children who were born here.

Local, state and Federal Governments spend about $11.8 billion a year educating legal and illegal immigrant children, according to the Urban Institute, a nonpartisan research organization, compared with the $227 billion spent to educate all children. Generally, this is more than offset by the taxes that legal and illegal immigrant families pay—$70.3 billion a year, the Urban Institute says—while receiving $42.9 billion in total services. Illegal immigrants pay $7 billion in taxes.

Maria T., however, represents the nightmare scenario— an illegal immigrant who's sucking money from the system and putting nothing back. Even so, it's not clear that she's a villain. She hopes one day to go to work herself. She hopes and believes that her bright children will become outstanding. She believes in America. . . .

Fears of Strangers

My wife, from Finland, has a green card; I'm English, in the process of applying for one myself; our son was born an American. When we moved into our house in Venice, Calif., one of our neighbors, an elderly white woman with whom we're now very friendly, said, "No Americans live on our block anymore."

Maybe she had the jitters about new neighbors, or maybe there was something else at play. I knew that her father had been born in Germany and had journeyed to Detroit, where she was born. I wanted to say that logically, therefore, our son is every bit as American as she is. But in any debate about nationality, I know, logic fades fast.

My own father once traced our family tree back to 1066, when one Baron de Rainier sailed from Normandy to help conquer England. Since then, give or take the occasional Irish excursion, my progenitors were all born within a hundred or so miles of one another in the north of England. So, when I came to America and found that nearly everyone was from somewhere else if they stepped back a generation or two, I found myself thrilled and oddly at ease. It explained America's drive, its generosity and up-for-anything energy. As (novelist Herman) Melville wrote, "We are not a nation, so much as a world."

Not everyone sees things this way. Many have drawn a line behind which they stand, *true* Americans, fearful and angry about the erosion of their identity. With unintended irony they talk of themselves as "natives." On immigration, they argue that enough is enough, that the borders must be secured and a drastic cutback enforced. Those who are allowed in, they say, must be professionals or skilled workers because the others—mobs of unskilled, third-world peasants—drain resources and take jobs. They cost billions and dilute the gene pool. They are mutating the face of America.

California itself, for instance, passed an anti-immigrant measure with scary ease. In 1994's state election nearly 60 percent voted for Proposition 187, the so-called Save-Our-State initiative, which sought to deny public education, nonemergency health care and welfare to illegal immigrants. By linking illegal immigration to joblessness and crime, Pete Wilson revived his flagging gubernatorial campaign and was swept back into office, even though, as an exit poll showed, few who voted for 187 actually thought it was going to work.

Wilson was avid for votes and a reaction and he got both. Many legal Latinos, fearful of deportation, refused to go near schools and emergency rooms. There was immigrant bashing and hate mail. Since the Republicans took control of the United States House and Senate, moreover, it seems as though all Washington has been grandstanding on the issue. Dozens of immigration-related bills were introduced. . . .

Many of the proposals are mean-spirited and, to a lot of

observers, wrongheaded. One would impose a tax on employers who hire *legal* aliens. Others would deny citizenship to children born in this country to illegals, or eliminate some categories of family immigration. The anti-immigration forces have done an excellent job of creating an atmosphere of crisis in which the debate has focused on *how* to slow the "flood" of immigration, legal and illegal. But illegal immigration should not be folded over to scapegoat legals as well. The real point is that there isn't any immigration crisis. . . .

How Many Immigrants?

"The perception is that immigration is out of control," says Joel Kotkin, author of "Tribes" and a fellow at the Pepperdine University Institute of Public Policy. "It isn't. If you say to most Americans, 'We have 800,000 legal immigrants a year,' they're going to reply, 'Hey, that's not so bad.' And this is the truth of the situation. But it's somehow been demonized so that people think there are millions coming across the border."

The Border Patrol logged 1,094,718 apprehensions in 1994. On page 26 of his "Alien Nation," a leading restrictionist, Peter Brimelow, writes that legal immigration is "overwhelmed by an estimated 2 to 3 million illegal entries into the country in every recent year." He goes on to note, correctly, that many of these illegal entrants go back home, and that some trundle to and fro across the border every day. By page 33, however, he's writing "a remarkable 2 to 3 million illegal immigrants may have succeeded in entering the country in 1993."

Within seven pages illegal entrants have mysteriously become illegal immigrants, attached to that hyperbolic two to three million, a figure vigorously disputed by I.N.S., which regards as preposterous the idea that for every border crosser caught another three get away. Indeed, throughout the 1970's there were some eight million border apprehensions and during that time, according to the best estimates of I.N.S., about one million illegals came to reside—eight apprehensions per illegal immigrant.

So how many illegals are coming in and staying each year now? The Urban Institute says 250,000 to 300,000. The Center for Immigration Studies, a conservative research group, says 400,000, while I.N.S. says 300,000. The Census Bureau until recently guessed 200,000 to 400,000; now it agrees with the I.N.S.

The 300,000 figure is considered firm because it was based on the years following 1988, when the I.N.S. started to process the genuinely reliable data it amassed following the 1986 amnesty for illegals. Too much of this and the eyes glaze over, but the gist is, the further you get from 1988, the flakier the statistics become. And the argument over the number of illegal immigrants is nothing compared with the furor over how much they cost.

Stop Scapegoating Illegal Immigrants

Arguing that illegal immigrants are the source of unemployment, higher taxes, and spiraling healthcare and social service costs . . . flies in the face of well-documented studies. For example, a 1992 U.S. Department of Justice study found that less than 1% of immigrants legalized under the 1986 amnesty had received general assistance, Social Security, SSI, worker's compensation or unemployment insurance. Less than one-half of 1% received food stamps or AFDC. As for jobs, it is well known that California's agriculture industry is dependent on immigrants, who overwhelmingly work at jobs that most U.S. citizens will not take because of the low pay, lack of benefits, and horrendous working conditions.

Rethinking Schools, Autumn 1994.

The fact is, no one knows for sure; there is simply no up-to-date research. "The issue has caught political fire," Papademetriou says. "But serious academics haven't got out into the field yet. They're reluctant to play into the hands of the politicians."

Immigration is in the spotlight not because of money but because it so impinges on issues like race, the role of government, national identity and change. Name an issue and you can hook it to immigration. One side looks at crime, failing schools and soaring welfare spending and sees too many immigrants. The other sees America, the greatest nation on earth, built on the backs of immigrants and still benefiting enormously from the brains, energy and determination (not to speak of low wages) of the next generation of newcomers. Right now the debate is more emotional than informed. It's all temper tantrums and red-hot sound bites.

Fear of Latinos

When people complain about immigration, about the alien "flood," it's Latin Americans they mean, who from their entry points in California and Miami are fanning out through the country. There's concern about the small minority who are criminals, and the seeming reluctance of these people to learn English. Mixed in with this is the prejudice summarized by D.H. Lawrence in "Mornings in Mexico." They are other, he concluded, they are dirty, I don't trust them and they stink. There's also the suggestion that Latinos are lazy, though everywhere you look in Los Angeles you see evidence to the contrary.

A Demand for Labor

Historically, immigration has been tolerated, even encouraged during labor shortages. Labor migration has been going on for centuries and it's hard to see how 300,000 or so illegal immigrants per year will make or break the American economy. Indeed, in Los Angeles they're most likely an asset. The number of illegals in California is thought to be growing by 125,000 a year—hardly an economic catastrophe in a state of 31 million. In Los Angeles, where 80,000 jobs were created last year, it's a definite plus. The city has a thirst for people who will work for $5 or even $3 an hour.

The legal Chinese immigrants who have revitalized the San Gabriel Valley, the Latinos who are opening businesses in depressed areas of South Los Angeles and the Russians and Iranians who are opening businesses all over are the principal reasons the city is so different from, say, Detroit. . . . Says Joel Kotkin: "The only place where American society is evolving is where the immigrant influx is strong. Cities would have no future without them. But if you're sitting in Idaho, it looks different.". . .

The Race Issue

Pro-immigration forces have tended to keep their focus tight on the economic issues because they sense that Americans don't want to be told they're racist. Nobody does. Yet, one of the problems with the immigration issue is that it *does* impinge on the race issue, and thus appeals temptingly and dangerously to the worst side of all of us.

A central argument of Brimelow's "Alien Nation" is that America has always had an essential nature, an ethnic core, and that it's white. He writes that "the first naturalization law, in 1790, stipulated that an applicant must be a 'free white person.' Blacks became full citizens only after the Civil War."

He goes on: "Maybe America should not have been like this. *But it was.*" And now: "Americans are being tricked out of their own identity."

Reading this, I'm overcome with a weird looking-glass giddiness. Someone's trying to change the rules here, to wipe a rag over history. America's identity is precisely that of mutation, its power drawn from an energetic and quite fearless ability to adapt and win. Its national book, after all, is "The Adventures of Huckleberry Finn," about a beautiful and dangerous river that never stops changing. . . .

An Immigrant Nation

America is an immigrant nation; indeed, a nation of strangers. I like it that way, though the arguments in favor of the idea are not merely sentimental and historical. Corporate interests value immigration for something that troubles us—keeping wages lower, and these days not just at the level of busboys and dayworkers.

The American economy is in relatively good shape and has pretty much the legal immigration it needs. The system isn't broken, doesn't need fixing—and certainly not in the ways that are now being proposed. Illegal immigration is touchier. Listening to academics makes it easy to forget the racially inflamed brush fire that is the debate in California.

Recent polls show a surprising sympathy even for illegal immigrants, provided they otherwise play by the rules: work, get documentation, learn English. Only 20 percent say immigrants take jobs away from citizens, and 69 percent say they do work that citizens don't necessarily want and that needs to be done. Few say that the American-born children of illegals should be deprived of education and welfare, let alone their citizenship. The message here is a sensible one: beef up the Border Patrol; deport criminals; don't break up families; target labor-enforcement at bad-guy sweatshop employers and make an effort to deal with temporary visa overstays, who surprisingly make up as much as 50 percent of all illegals; supply Federal assistance to heavily impacted areas such as Los Angeles, and forget the idea of a national verification system or an identification card.

Ultimately, this is a debate about values, not money. This is about how America feels about itself.

"New immigrants, often illegal newcomers, . . . will work for substandard wages."

Illegal Immigrants Harm America's Economy and Workers

Federation for American Immigration Reform

Most observers agree that the primary motivation for illegal immigration in America is the lure of jobs. However, they disagree on what effect immigrants have on the economy and on American workers with whom they may compete for employment. In the following viewpoint by the Federation for American Immigration Reform (FAIR), illegal immigrants are blamed for causing unemployment and hardship for American workers because of their willingness to work for low wages. FAIR is a national lobbying group that works to stop illegal immigration and limit legal immigration.

As you read, consider the following questions:

1. What role do subcontractors play in displacing American workers, according to FAIR?
2. What examples of job loss due to immigration does the author provide?
3. According to FAIR, why are politicians not concerned about worker displacement?

From "Immigration and Job Displacement," by Federation for American Immigration Reform, *FAIR Issue Brief*, October 1999. Copyright © 1999 by the Federation for American Immigration Reform. Reprinted with permission.

O ne of the overlooked ways in which immigration harms the American workforce is displacement, that is, when established workers, whether natives or immigrants, lose their jobs to new immigrants, often illegal newcomers, who will work for substandard wages.

Sometimes the employer intentionally replaces natives with foreigners to have a cheaper, more easily exploited workforce. Sometimes the displacement comes through an intermediary. In these cases, work is let out to subcontractors. The firms that use immigrants—and pay them low wages—underbid the firms that use natives. In some cases, the ultimate employer may not even be aware that native workers have been displaced. Regardless, the effects on Americans are real; as the Immigration and Naturalization Service put it:

> The critical potential negative impacts of immigrants are displacement of incumbent worker groups from their jobs and wage depression for those who remain in the affected sectors.

The web of complex interactions among factory openings and closings, choice of production methods, ethnic networking in hiring, and labor subcontracting make it difficult to prove iron-clad demonstrations of displacement. Yet such evidence does abound.

Cases of Displacement

Another clear case of displacement happened in the tomato industry in the 1980s. A group of unionized legal border crossers picked the tomato crop for many years in San Diego County, and were making $4.00 an hour in 1980. In the 1980s, growers switched to a crew of illegal aliens and lowered the wage to $3.35. Almost all the veteran workers who were unwilling to work at the reduced rate disappeared from the tomato fields.

Sometimes those displaced by new foreign workers are other foreign workers. In the raisin grape industry of California, Mestizos (the Spanish-speaking population of Mexico were laid off and replaced with lower cost Mixtecs (the indigenous people of Mexico). According to a study of the industry, the Mixtecs "have driven the Mestizos out of the market."

Agriculture has many other instances of employers' switching to immigrant workers (legal and illegal) to increase their profits. For example, Hispanic migrants have displaced native black workers in the Georgia peach industry and migrants have replaced natives and previous immigrants in the cucumber and apple industries in Michigan. The melon industry found it possible to replace unionized crews of mostly native workers doing manual packing in the field with lower-paid Mexican field crews in tandem with the introduction of mechanized packing houses.

In the furniture industry, competition from immigrant-laden plants in Southern California, closed all the unionized plants in the San Francisco area and removed natives from the workforce in favor of lesser-paid aliens.

In the last twenty years, the meatpacking industry has completely reorganized around the use of immigrant rather than native labor. IBP, the nation's leading meatpacking company, now recruits workers from Mexico and directly along the border. As a result, the proportion of the labor force protected by union contracts and the share of natives in meat processing has dropped dramatically.

Unions fall before the weight of imported labor. In the Mission Foods tortilla factory strike, management lowered wages by 40 percent, and when the native labor went on strike, the Mexican managers intentionally brought in recent immigrant strikebreakers to replace them. Some of the natives returned to work at the reduced wages, but most left.

Similar phenomena have swept over the hotel industry as well, with immigrant workers displacing native black workers *en masse*. In Los Angeles, unionized black janitors had been earning $12 an hour, with benefits. But, with the advent of subcontractors who compose roaming crews of Mexican and El Salvadoran laborers, the pay dropped to the then minimum wage of $3.35 an hour. Within two years, the unionized crews had all been displaced by the foreign ones, and without any skills, the native force did not as a rule, find new work.

Wage Depression

Many politicians and some citizens do not concern themselves with such displacement since it affects primarily low-skilled Americans, who tend to lack political clout. As a re-

Costs of Immigration

"Immigration policy has been captured by special interests who peddle the notion that immigration is an unmitigated benefit to the nation and that it is costless," says Vernon M. Briggs Jr., a professor at Cornell University. "Nothing could be further from the truth." According to Briggs, the national unemployment rate in 1997 (the last year for which figures are available) was 4.9 percent; for the foreign born, it was 7.4 percent; for the foreign-born without a high-school education, it was 9.8 percent; and for native-born unskilled workers, it was 14.5 percent. Thus, concludes Briggs, there is no shortage of unskilled workers in the nation and no need to import them. What's more, importing the unskilled has the greatest impact on the least skilled segment of the labor force "that is already having the greatest difficulty finding employment."

Blacks are hit hardest, reports Frank L. Morris Sr., retired dean of Morgan State University's graduate school. Competition with immigrants "has been devastating for African-Americans in high-immigration states," particularly among farm workers, janitors, security guards, taxi drivers, child-care workers and those employed in construction, restaurant and hotel jobs, Morris said during congressional testimony. Furthermore, "Many African-American citizens [in places where there is high immigration] are living in dire straits. I consistently confront the myth that immigrants take jobs that other Americans such as African-Americans do not want. . . . African-American workers and especially young urban workers were and are being denied opportunities in construction that were given to immigrant construction workers."

August Gribbin, *Insight on the News*, September 20, 1999.

sult, immigration has been responsible for forty to fifty percent of the wage depression in recent decades. Some research estimates that nearly two million Americans a year are displaced by immigration.

Americans deserve decent jobs at decent wages, not unfair competition from imported foreign workers who are exploited to the point of indentured servitude. We need immigration reform to stop the massive influx of foreign workers from doing further harm to the living standard of our low-skilled fellow citizen and legal resident workers.

*"Illegal immigration has turned out to be a
great boon for the American economy."*

Illegal Immigrants Do Not Harm America's Economy or Workers

Robert Scheer

Robert Scheer is a syndicated columnist and former national correspondent for the *Los Angeles Times*. In the viewpoint that follows, he contends that illegal immigrants do not depress wages or create unemployment for American workers, but in fact are a boon to the U.S. economy. He calls for an amnesty or legalization of the status of currently illegal workers as a way of improving their situation and keeping labor standards in America from eroding.

As you read, consider the following questions:

1. Why has the AFL-CIO, a labor union, reversed its prior opposition to illegal immigrant labor, according to Scheer?
2. Why does the author support the increase of the minimum wage?
3. What benefits would a general amnesty for undocumented workers bring, as explained by Scheer?

Time to cheer the much-maligned illegal alien. Illegal immigration has turned out to be a great boon for the American economy. Dire predictions that the millions of workers who crossed illegally into this country would depress wages and increase unemployment have proved to be incorrect.

Indeed, not only has the economy grown to unprecedented levels, but unemployment is at its lowest point in decades. It is an impending labor shortage that is the great concern of economists, as reflected in the remarks of Federal Reserve Chairman Alan Greenspan.

In February 2000, the AFL-CIO [labor union] dropped the historic opposition of the trade unions to illegal immigrant labor and called for Congress to repeal the law that makes it a crime for employers to hire undocumented workers. This call, supported by many business leaders as well, is a recognition that immigrant workers are vital to the productivity of many sectors of the economy, not to mention an important new source of union membership.

Absorbing Immigrant Workers

The productive contribution of immigrant labor and the need for more not less in the future challenges the assertion behind legislation such as the infamous Proposition 187, passed in 1994 in California, that illegal immigrants represent a drain on the economy. Such measures seek to cut social services to immigrants, including educational opportunities for their children. But the buoyant economy supports the view that immigrants pay more in taxes than they receive in social services.

It also bolsters the case for another general amnesty for immigrants who are here illegally in order to allow them to become legally documented workers and eventually U.S. citizens. The last such amnesty was granted by Congress more than a decade ago [in 1986]. The strength of the U.S. economy since supports the view that those people, 6 million total, have been easily absorbed into mainstream life as productive citizens.

The Immigration and Naturalization Service estimates that the number of illegal workers is now at the same level as at the time of the previous amnesty. Clearly, if their status is made legal, these workers could be just as easily absorbed into the economy.

Once workers are here legally, they can act to improve their circumstances by asserting their rights to join labor unions and to otherwise ensure that U.S. labor standards are not eroded. In the process, this country, with its booming economy, could provide a model for the world that workers need not be exploited in the name of national prosperity. As it is now, and as the AFL-CIO resolution noted, the laws against immigrants allow some employers to "knowingly exploit a worker's undocumented status in order to prevent enforcement of workplace protection laws."

A proposal to raise the minimum wage, still stalled in Congress, would be the most effective means of ensuring that the 260,000 new immigrant workers who illegally enter the country each year do not erode labor standards. The evidence is overwhelming that the most recent increase in the minimum wage did not, as opponents predicted, lead to a loss of jobs but contributed to a more stable work force.

It is a truism to speak of the U.S. as part of a world economy and consequently unrealistic to expect that the flow of workers will not parallel the trade of goods and commerce. Images of the good life in this country have become the staple cultural diet of moviegoers and television watchers throughout the world. Migration to this and other prosperous countries has proved impossible to stop.

Increase Immigration Quotas

But what we can ensure is that those who enter this country to work conform to rather than erode the labor standards that have taken centuries to enshrine in law. If the pay is good and the working conditions decent and we still need more workers, then let them come.

Ultimately the answer is to loosen the immigration quotas so that legal immigration becomes a realistic possibility for those now forced to enter the country illegally. That is particularly obvious as applies to Mexico, which still produces the bulk of illegal immigrants, because the chances for legal immigration from that country are kept ridiculously slim by low quotas.

In the meantime, we should reward those who, like our own parents and grandparents, managed to overcome many obstacles to enter this country and make it the great place that it is. A general amnesty for those undocumented immigrants who have been living stable, hard-working lives under difficult circumstances would be an excellent way to honor the memory of our ancestors while guaranteeing that our economy has the labor force needed for another decade of unprecedented growth.

"'Invasion' is a word frequently heard along the border, and official statistics show why."

Illegal Immigration Harms Border Communities

Glynn Custred

Glynn Custred is a professor of anthropology at California State University at Hayward. In the following viewpoint, he examines how American communities bordering Mexico have been adversely affected by illegal immigration. He blames illegal immigrants for increased instances of litter, property vandalism, crime, drug smuggling, and other problems. Efforts to stop illegal immigration in places like San Diego, California, and El Paso, Texas, have resulted in new immigration problems in adjoining areas. Custred writes that rural property owners who have taken action against illegal immigrants have been improperly criticized.

As you read, consider the following questions:
1. How many illegal immigrants cross the U.S.-Mexico border, according to Custred?
2. What have been the effects of immigration enforcement efforts such as Operation Gatekeeper, according to the author?
3. What relationship exists between illegal immigration and drug smuggling, according to Custred?

Excerpted from "Alien Crossings," by Glynn Custred, *The American Spectator*, October 2000. Copyright © 2000 by *The American Spectator*. Reprinted with permission.

Olga Robles and her husband Frank live just eight blocks from the international boundary that separates Douglas, Arizona, from the Mexican city of Agua Prieta. For years men have illegally crossed the border on their way north looking for work. Mrs. Robles said she frequently saw them pass through town in pairs or in small groups. Then about two years ago the trickle swelled to a flood with groups of thirty to well over a hundred people at a time pouring across the border, hurrying through alleys, through people's yards and between their houses, climbing over roofs and clambering over graves in the cemetery. They knocked down fences, trampled flowers and shrubs, and cluttered neighborhoods with litter. They came in groups all day long and in a steady stream throughout the night while dogs in town barked till dawn. In frustration Mrs. Robles finally told the authorities, "If you can't do anything about the trespassers, then at least shoot the dogs so I can get some sleep."

Besides the surging numbers Mrs. Robles noticed something else. No longer were the migrants just men looking for work; now there were women and children as well, whole families illegally crossing and streaming north. "That's when I realized it was an invasion," she said. Indeed "invasion" is a word frequently heard along the border, and official statistics show why. In the first six months of this year, the U.S. border patrol apprehended 176,655 illegal aliens in the 21-mile Douglas section of the border alone.

There is no accurate way of extrapolating from those figures how many people actually made it across, since for every one illegal apprehended the border patrol estimates that three to five get away. The same individual may be apprehended more than once before finally getting in. But according to think tank and government experts, since 1983 about half a million a year have managed to enter the United States illegally along the southern border.

Illegal Immigration in El Paso and San Diego

Before 1994 the urban corridors of El Paso, Texas and San Diego, California accounted for two-thirds of the illegal entries. San Diego was the most notorious, and it was in California that the volume eventually produced a political reaction.

The international boundary in San Diego sharply separates the teeming residential sprawl of the Mexican city of Tijuana from the undeveloped canyons and ravines of the southern end of San Diego. For years this neglected zone was a dangerous no man's land known for its lawlessness and violence. Illegal entrants were robbed every night and often raped and murdered by Mexican bandits and sometimes by Mexican policemen or criminals operating under their protection. The flavor of those violent times has been caught by Joseph Wambaugh in *Lines and Shadows*, a factual account of border crime in the 1970's and of the special unit formed by the San Diego Police Department in a futile attempt to combat it.

Throughout the 1980's and early 90's the 14-mile stretch of border in San Diego was hostile, violent, and out of control. Border patrol agents use terms like "chaos" and "anarchy" to describe it, saying that they faced riot conditions every night. Crowds would gather on the Tijuana side and pelt border-patrol agents with rocks. Shots were sometimes fired across the border at patrolling agents, and almost daily thousands of Mexicans would gather on the U.S. side, then dash forward en masse in what were known as banzai runs.

The influx of illegal aliens into southern California, and its mounting cost to taxpayers, spawned a political reaction. It took the form of a popular initiative, Proposition 187, which would deny public services to anyone residing illegally in the state. The same public sentiment that assured an overwhelming victory for Prop. 187 in 1994 (with 59 percent of the vote) also resuscitated Gov. Pete Wilson's flagging re-election campaign, eventually carrying him to victory.

It was in El Paso, however, that the first attempt to regain control of the border was undertaken. In 1994 Silvester Reyes, then chief of the El Paso sector of the border patrol and now a U.S. congressman, devised a plan called Operation Blockade, later renamed Hold the Line. It focused not on apprehension once illegals had crossed the border, but rather on deterring them from trying to cross in the first place. Operation Hold the Line combined fences, technology, and close monitoring by agents stationed along the border. The result was a significant drop in illegal entry and other crimes in the El Paso area.

That same year similar measures were taken in San Diego under the name of Operation Gatekeeper. There too illegal entry was sharply reduced and crime dropped, not only in the border zone itself but for the entire San Diego area. Another effect of Gatekeeper, however, was that illegal migration simply flowed to the east beyond the reach of Gatekeeper, spilling into the eastern part of San Diego County, thus creating problems for rural property owners there. People all along the border call this the balloon effect: Squeeze it in one place and it bulges in another. Cut down the flow of illegals in El Paso or San Diego, and it moves to places like Douglas and from there to ranch lands and ever deeper into the desert beyond. In other words, despite relief in the urban corridors the overall problem remains unsolved. The border patrol, which apprehended a record 1.6 million illegal entrants in fiscal 1999, says it's "on pace" to exceed that number in fiscal 2000.

Incentives for Immigration

The incentive for migration into the United States is the availability of low-skill jobs here and poverty, low wages, and an expanding population in Mexico and Central America. What helps drive it, though, are networks created and maintained between expatriate communities in the U.S. and their home towns and regions abroad. Expatriate communities serve to attract, support, and absorb newcomers, thus providing an important part of the magnet that pulls them north. This population transfer would not be possible without the existence of an organized and lucrative smuggling industry involving millions of dollars each year.

Illegal migrants do not simply show up at the border and then cross over. They first arrange a reception with friends and relatives in the U.S. who line up jobs for them and who often advance them the cost of the trip. The migrant or his U.S. relatives or friends then contract with a smuggler not only for the border crossing itself, but also for safe houses and necessary transportation along the way. Women and children are sometimes brought to the border in cattle trucks, and on the U.S. side aliens are often packed into vans like sardines. In Douglas, Arizona, a town of 15,000, there's been a sudden rise in taxi services.

The current cost for illegal entry is said to be $1,500 a head. For Central Americans the cost and risk are even greater, since they must first illegally cross Mexico's southern border, and then clandestinely travel the entire length of that country before arriving at the U.S. border. Mexico has strict immigration laws of its own and does not want aliens working illegally in the country. When caught, the alien sometimes suffers abuse at the hands of Mexican police that would not be tolerated in the U.S.

A County Sheriff's View of Immigrants

The citizens of Cochise County [in Arizona] are experiencing a challenge of unprecedented proportions. Each month, tens of thousands of illegal immigrants from all over the world pour across the 83 miles of international border we share with Mexico. . . .

Virtually everyone who lives in or visits our area has been impacted by this mess in a very personal way. Our fences are cut, our water sources damaged or destroyed, our properties littered with tons of garbage, clothing and human waste. The San Pedro Riparian Area, designated by the federal government as critical habitat for several endangered species is so contaminated with this garbage that it may never recover. The same is true of our national parks, national forests, wildlife refuge and state and private properties as well.

Moms and dads can't leave their kids at school bus stops. Our highways are rendered dangerous by inexperienced drivers in unsafe vehicles. Hundreds of trespasses against our homes, our properties and upon our cherished quality of life occur daily. In some places we cannot even go out for a morning or evening walk without fear and trepidation. These are not conditions that are acceptable anywhere, much less in what should be a peaceful and tranquil rural American environment.

Larry Dever, testimony before the U.S. Senate Judiciary Subcommittee on Immigration, June 27, 2000.

Once established in this country and employed in some low-paying job, the illegal alien usually lives frugally, often no better than at home, until he has paid off his debt. He then generally contributes to the entry of others in the same way he himself has entered. Thus as migrant communities grow in the United States the magnet for illegal immigration becomes more powerful. And as more money is pumped into the smuggling enterprise, that illegal industry continues to thrive and grow.

Douglas Becomes a Corridor

As a commercial activity, alien smuggling is sensitive to the business climate. Once Hold the Line and Gatekeeper made crossing in urban areas more difficult, smugglers eventually identified Douglas as a corridor through which the trade could be channeled with much less risk. The town lies on the Pan American Highway that connects the interiors of Mexico and the United States. Its "twin city" Agua Prieta on the Mexican side provides a convenient staging ground for illegal crossing. Those advantages, together with a lightly guarded border, turned unsuspecting Douglas in 1994 into the main crossing point of a massive and lucrative international smuggling operation. As one journalist observed, the authorities and citizens of that small border town were suddenly confronted by a "global population shift passing through their back yards" for which none of them was prepared.

The mob scene through Douglas finally ceased once a strengthened and illuminated fence was erected, and once the border patrol had beefed up its presence in town. The stream of migrants, however, did not stop but simply flowed around Douglas, mainly to the west where ranch lands with water tanks and a network of roads facilitate this kind of mass smuggling operation. Ranchers and other rural property owners then began to experience what the rural population of eastern San Diego County experienced a few years earlier. The ranchers complained about fences broken daily by crowds of migrants, about gates left open leaving cattle free to stray, about cattle that were killed, watchdogs poisoned, water tanks drained, buildings broken into, and property stolen. One rancher estimates that the cost of constant repairs has run into tens of thousands of dollars. And everywhere there is the trash: piles of empty plastic water bottles, food wrappers, dirty diapers, clothing, feces, toilet paper, anything left by masses of people on the move. Indeed if you saw nothing but the litter you could well believe that a mass migration is underway.

The cost and bother of constant trespass and the fear of theft and burglary have meant that many rural people in Cochise County, where Douglas is located, are now arming themselves. Warning shots have been fired and many are worried that something worse might happen. What frightens the ranchers most, however, is not the aliens but rather drug smugglers. These are well-armed men, some carrying fully automatic weapons. Ranchers in both San Diego and Cochise Counties have reported seeing armed men on the U.S. side of the border, military in appearance, dressed in black, and armed with automatic rifles.

Some believe that they are from the Mexican army acting in support of smugglers. Whether they are or not, however, Mexican army units and armed police are frequently reported entering U.S. territory, a violation that evokes angry response when U.S. authorities stray across the border into Mexico. Ron Sanders was for five years the chief of the Tucson sector of the border patrol until his retirement in August 1999. Hardly a month goes by, he said, without some kind of incursion by Mexican police or military. Sometimes shooting is involved. He recalls an armed stand-off on the U.S. side of the border between the Nogales police and the Mexican army.

The latest publicized incursion took place in March 2000 near Santa Teresa, New Mexico. Two Mexican army Humvees penetrated more than a mile into the United States and fired on a mounted border patrolman and on a border-patrol vehicle. The soldiers were detained but were later returned to Mexico along with their weapons. There was no official protest from Washington, even though firing on a U.S. law officer is a felony offense.

Drug Smugglers

Drug smugglers often use lonely and difficult trails through the mountains, or go on horseback through more remote parts of the desert. At times they mingle with groups of aliens, or follow them for cover. On occasion they also use aliens as "mules" to carry drugs across the border in payment for their passage. One rancher near Douglas tells of a young illegal who knocked at a neighbor's door one night.

The young man had slipped away from his group because its guide had forced them all to carry illicit drugs. Fearing they might all end up killed, he ran to the nearest house begging the rancher to call the police.

As the situation near Douglas worsened, some of the ranchers decided to take action on their own. Roger Barnett owns a 22,000-acre ranch outside Douglas. Soon he and his brother Don, like his neighbor Larry Vance and others, began rounding up aliens on their property and holding them until the border patrol arrived to arrest them. Advocacy groups howled in protest, as did the Mexican government. Their lawyers demanded that the ranchers be prosecuted for false arrest, kidnapping, intimidation, criminal assault, violation of civil rights, in short anything lawyers can come up with to advance their clients' interests. Larry Vance retorted that "the only rights that have been violated are those of American citizens whose privacy, property, and nation are invaded from Mexico."

Rosario Green, Mexico's foreign minister, voiced concern about the "intolerant expression of some American ranchers who promote the persecution of migrants along the border." Green declared a "red alert," and the Mexican government hired Washington lawyers to look into the possibility of a civil suit against the ranchers. All the while the Mexican press demonized the ranchers as "racist xenophobic vigilantes" who hunted down innocent Mexican migrants like animals. Vance emphasizes that nobody blames the aliens, nobody's mad at them, and nobody hates them. In fact, his father came from Mexico in 1939, as did Olga Robles's grandparents in 1903. Indeed many residents of Cochise County are of Mexican descent. The problem is not one of race or nationality, but of violations of the rights of American citizens by an illegal enterprise acting in the United States from Mexican territory.

Environment Concerns

Rural property owners in Cochise County are not the only U.S. citizens affected by the mass smuggling of drugs and aliens. A hundred miles farther west lies the Tohono O'odham (formerly the Papago) Indian reservation, which shares a 71-

mile border with Mexico. It is the second largest reservation in the country, with a population of 22,000 scattered over a million square miles of scrub brush and tall, graceful Sahuaro cactus.

Larry Seligman is chief of the Tohono O'odham police. Like his counterparts in neighboring border communities he complains about the large numbers of illegals crossing his jurisdiction. They come in groups of well over a hundred, he says, the largest he has encountered numbering one hundred sixty-four. Like the ranchers of Cochise County, those Tohono O'odham living near the border are afraid to leave their homes for fear of break-ins, and those living along the migrant trails are disturbed by the crowds passing only yards from their homes, "violating their space" as Seligman puts it, and leaving the inevitable trail of trash behind them. The Tohono O'odham revere the environment, says Seligman, and are especially offended when they see it defiled in this manner.

The National Park Service also reveres the environment. Its credo is "to preserve and protect." There are two national parks along the border in Arizona: the Coronado National Memorial in Cochise County, which runs nearly three and a half miles along the border, and the Organ Pipe Cactus National Monument adjacent to the Tohono O'odham reservation, which shares a 31-mile border with Mexico. Jim Bellamy, superintendent of the Coronado National Memorial, says that the passage of illegals in the park area has increased by some 300 percent in the last two years. Such large numbers not only threaten the reserve, he says, but in the case of drug smuggling, pose a potential hazard to visitors and park personnel.

William Wellman, superintendent of Organ Pipe, estimates that 40,000 to 80,000 illegals passed through the national memorial last year. Although most of the land is designated wilderness, Wellman told the Associated Press that "it's hard to go anywhere and not see evidence of trash. We pick it up by the hundreds." Monument spokeswoman Mitzi Frank says that smugglers drive through the fragile desert in cars unsuited for the country. They get stuck and the Park Service has to call tow trucks to remove the abandoned vehicles, thus further damaging the environment. All along the migrant routes vegetation is trampled and the soil is compacted resulting in scars to the landscape that will last for centuries.

If all this is hard on the environment and on U.S. citizens, it can be far worse on the migrants themselves. Once they get to the border they are helpless in a strange and hostile environment, often suffering from bandits on the Mexican side and sometimes abandoned on the U.S. side by their guides, not knowing where they are, how to deal with the desert they must traverse, nor what to do next except walk northward in the murderous hundred-degree heat, hoping that far-off Phoenix lies just over the next hill. Tohono O'odham Police Chief Seligman says that his patrols have found people wearing street clothes and street shoes wandering helpless in the desert, who ran to police begging for water.

Some migrants, however, do not make it. Some have drowned trying to cross the Rio Grande River in Texas or the All America Canal in California; others have died of cold in the mountains in winter or of dehydration in the desert; still others are injured or die in accidents in overcrowded vans carrying them north from the border. Official border-patrol figures show that migrant deaths along the southern border from October 1, 1998 to July 21, 2000 total 756. That figure will certainly have grown by summer's end.

What Should Be Done

Some despair of ever getting control of the border. Others, however, are convinced the number of illegals could be greatly reduced with the right combination of fences, all-weather roads, technology, and adequate staffing adapted in different mixes to the different environments of the border. But these measures would only work if backed up by mobile patrols behind the border and by interior enforcement. This means regular worksite inspection, worker validation, employer sanctions, and deportations. Such an integrated and consistent policy would send the message through the migrant networks that illegal entry is risky and that apprehension is a strong possibility once across the border.

"The Border Patrol destabilizes the community."

Enforcement of Immigration Laws Harms Border Communities

Maria Jiménez, interviewed by Nic Paget-Clarke

Maria Jiménez is director of the Immigration Law Enforcement Monitoring Project (ILEMP), an organization that works with local communities on the U.S.-Mexico border to challenge human rights abuses in the enforcement of immigration law. The following viewpoint is excerpted from a 1998 interview of Jiménez by Nic Paget-Clarke, publisher of *In Motion Magazine*, an online multicultural publication. Jiménez asserts that communities along the border are being destabilized and otherwise harmed by the actions of the Border Patrol and other federal agents sent to capture illegal immigrants. Illegal immigration laws, she argues, create a "war zone" atmosphere in border communities and contribute to the oppression of poor migrants for the benefit of the wealthy.

As you read, consider the following questions:
1. How are attitudes toward people of Mexican descent affected by immigration laws, according to Jiménez?
2. In what respects are Border Patrol units similar to the slave patrols that were common in the South during slavery, according to the author?
3. What examples of community harm by immigration law enforcement does Jiménez provide?

In Motion Magazine: At what point did you realize you were going to start using the word 'militarization'?

Maria Jiménez: Immediately. The first thing I did when I was hired [by ILEMP] in April of '87 was to do document research of what the problem was. I wrote an article for the National Immigration Project newsletter called "The Militarization of the Border". It was immediate that the context of our work would be this. One, because of the large number of not only Border Patrol agents and Immigration and Naturalization Service (INS) concentrated on the border, but also numerous federal agencies. Currently about 46 federal agencies work on the border. Secondly, we had already begun to see sectors speaking about the use of the military directly. There were even some laws like the 1986 law which authorized the use of military bases for keeping undocumented people.

Even though we won many battles in the area of accountability, the area of holding individual agents accountable for their actions as well as targeting policies and being able to get recommendations we were making accepted, in the area of a de-militarized border—we were losing the war. . . .

There was the view that problems come from south of the border. Statistically, the Urban Institute in '94 indicated that out of ten undocumented people in the United States only four crossed the southern border, but the national view is that everybody who is undocumented comes through the southern border. Again the Urban Institute found that out of 100 undocumented people in the United States only 39%, the INS says 55%, are Mexican nationals. Yet 90% of the people arrested are Mexican nationals, and 85% of the resources to deal with "the undocumented problem" are placed in communities along the U.S.-Mexico border. That problem, the problem of the national perception of viewing the border as a war zone and immigrants as enemies and subsequently border communities—you can conclude when you have military patrols in your town that somehow somebody thought you were the enemies of this country—that was why we were losing. . . .

In Motion Magazine: It does seem ironic that at the same time as we have free trade which you would think would make the border more open, the border is actually being closed. How do you explain that?

Maria Jiménez: I don't think it's an irony. I think it's a function of the global system in which the decisions are being made by transnational corporations and by entities that are not democratic. When we look at the function of mobility across the border we must look at that global system. The United Nations says there are five billion people in the world. Two billion are in the labor market, and of those something like 125 million are actually people who live outside of their countries of origin. The U.S. receives 1% annually of these migrants. Each year, since the '80s, there's been an increase in the number of refugees, people who move across international borders because of natural disasters or civil strife. There [are] also economic migrants, people who move to incorporate themselves into labor markets. Of these there are about a million a year.

When you look at the scheme of globalization and restructuring one sees that the economic and political elites of the world have no problems in getting across borders. The CEO's, wealthy refugees—we saw the case of Kuwait—can easily come into the United States. If you are in a political elite you have no problem moving back and forth legally between countries. The militarized borders, the walls, the agents, are really to impede the mobility of the international working poor who attempt to cross borders. In that sense border politics for me is a strategic aspect of economic development policy apparent in our global system. It's a policy that seeks to create a world of low wages and high profits.

When you regulate labor but do not regulate capital then you create the conditions of: 1) attempting to immobilize populations that are left in countries to which you can move your assembly plants and pay workers very low wages. And 2) if people can get across illegally into your country then the illegality creates the conditions for a group of people who are socially disenfranchised, politically disenfranchised, and economically vulnerable. They are placed in industries where again the motive is low wages and high profits.

The only comparison I can make on the issue of mobility in the United States is during the slavery period in the

South. I think one of the first police forces to be paid by governments were the famous slave patrols of the South. The function of the slave patrols was to impede the mobility of the slaves and to insure that if one did escape a plantation that person would be returned. This reinforced the existing social and economic structure. It's in the same sense that we have a Border Patrol and the INS. We have a police force whose function is to reinforce immobility, to reinforce the conditions that maximize profits and ensure low wages. . . .

Border Patrol Abuses

In recent years, Amnesty International, Americas Watch and other human rights organizations have documented numerous other incidents in which unarmed men, women and children have been fired upon, beaten, sexually abused, deprived of food, water and medical treatment, maimed and killed by Border Patrol agents or federal troops assigned to the U.S.-Mexico border. While immigration authorities attempt to portray this growing violence against both legal and illegal immigrants as well as U.S.-born Latinos as a collection of isolated incidents, evidence suggests that this trend is the product of relatively recent transformations within the Border Patrol itself.

Since its founding in 1924, the Border Patrol's purpose has ostensibly been to prevent the entry of unauthorized persons and materials into U.S. territory. Over the last decade, however, its mission has been expanded to preventing the entry of terrorists and drugs into the country. This expansion of institutional objectives has, in turn, led to a dramatic militarization of both its ideology and its policing practices, prompting the direct involvement of the U.S. military in the patrolling of the border. As official concerns shifted towards the protection the national territory from the allegedly foreign threats of terrorism and drugs, federal authorities have increasingly turned towards military strategy as a way to control the influx of "dangerous" peoples into United States.

Carol Nagengast, *Report on the Americas*, November/December 1998.

Of all the labor laws of the United States—violations of safety and health, violations of minimum wage, violations of the use of toxic entities in plants, of all the violations of laws between labor and management—none of these are enforced by a group of armed individuals who come to your work site to make sure that you comply with these laws. The only area is the area of the . . . authorized or unauthorized worker.

That's why I think it's similar to the slave patrols of the South. Why is it so important in our economic system to have armed agents come into a work site to enforce this? That's what gives me the impression that it's a key area that ensures and reinforces the existing inequalities on an international level. It guarantees for the transnational corporate strategy the mechanism of low wages, high profits.

That's why it's not illogical. It's illogical from our view because what we seek is justice for all sectors of the world politic. Many times I talk about the idea that the real issue in border politics is the issue of equality of border mobility. Border mobility is not equal. The wealthy can go all over the world without any problem.

In Motion Magazine: So the work of the Border Patrol is not so much to keep Mexican workers out of the United States as to keep them being available for work in Mexico?

Maria Jiménez: And highly exploited if they do cross. We saw this for example with the incident of the deaf people who were brought from Mexico to New York and who literally lived in slave conditions. . . .

In Motion Magazine: What is the relationship between the Border Patrol and the Houston police?

Maria Jiménez: In Houston, . . . the organization of Spanish-speaking officers . . . pushed so that there would be an internal regulation in the City of Houston in which the local police and the local city jails would not be associated with the INS. The officers argued that this was not about less enforcement but about more effective local law enforcement. That is, if the major component of community-oriented policing is gaining the confidence and trust of the population that you police, and if your role is more of peace officer and the idea that you should be using more of the skills of arbitration and conciliation and less of the tough cop mentality, then that trust and that confidence is immediately eroded in the immigrant population if you associate with the INS. This regulation would show to the immigrant population that public safety and police protection are there for them as well. That they could access these services.

This is critical in the case of domestic violence. Many times all the woman wants is for the man to stop the abuse. She does not necessarily want him to be charged or for herself or him to be deported. If she knows she or he are going to be deported she's not going to report him.

The same thing is true for other forms of abuse. For example, an undocumented group of Mexican and Honduran workers went to protest the fact that a contractor had robbed them of wages. This contractor took out a gun and began shooting at them. He shot one of them in the foot. The injured man was taken to a hospital. When the security guard at the hospital insinuated that if the worker did not give the name of the contractor to him he would call the INS the worker left the hospital untreated. This indicates the degree of fear of local authorities reporting to the INS that makes the immigrant population more vulnerable to crime and to the lack of reporting of crime.

So this is the current policy in Houston. But under current immigration law within the counter-terrorism act it is now authorized that a local jurisdiction can ask the Attorney General to be deputized as INS agents. As far as I know Salt Lake City is one of the first cities to do this. From our perspective, because we've learned from the Spanish-speaking officers here in Houston, this is a serious situation regarding public safety for everyone. It's not about less enforcement but about more effective enforcement at the local levels. People won't report crimes or help in an investigation. It leaves a whole group of people vulnerable to the criminal element. This is a deterioration of the community per se.

Community Impacts

In Motion Magazine: What is the long-term impact on the community of the constant presence of the Border Patrol?

Maria Jiménez: Often when I address Mexican-origin audiences in the United States, I talk about how we are the only ethnic group in the whole country who can claim to have a national police force we can call our very own.

When I've addressed Border Patrol agents, because I have addressed them at a couple of training sessions, I tell them about the complexity of our relationship, given that policy has thrown us together. It wasn't their choice to police us. It is policy that has placed them in the position of policing us. We are the police constituency. There's a whole folklore about it. There's songs, there's jokes, there's stories. And the jokes particularly are revealing. Sometimes the agent is the butt of the joke, sometimes it's the immigrant, sometimes it's both of them together.

I tell them about *La Jornada*, one of the most widely-read newspapers in Mexico. Every Sunday has a cartoon column called "When the Border Patrol Catches Up with Me". The Border Patrol is such an ingrained part of our existence in the United States, I tell them, I can't imagine living in the United States without the INS. They are part of our existence.

There was an old (INS) sector chief who retired in El Paso and a reporter from Juarez told me that he asked him "What do you think of Mexicans?" He said, "I know them very well. I've been arresting them for 25 years." And the same is true for us, we who have been arrested. We are always confronting them. In that sense there is a complex relationship developed with them.

Some were surprised that people weren't afraid to go to the INS offices during amnesty. A Mexican wouldn't be surprised. Why? Because when you know them, you know both their good and their bad. . . .

By the same token, our detention facilities are staffed 90% by Latinos and Mexican-origin people. Why? Well, part of it is the poverty, that's the job that is available. But the second thing is the familiarity. I coined a phrase—the abused-community syndrome—like the battered-wife syndrome. It's gone on for so many generations that we no longer see the abuse. It's become a way of life. Part of our work is increasing public awareness that we are an abused community. This doesn't happen to other communities. Particularly the issue of U.S. citizens being stopped, and questioned and detained, and sometimes even deported. It doesn't happen to Anglo Americans, African Americans. It happens to Americans of Mexican origin.

When I address Mexican American audiences I talk to them about the fact that even in our own self-definition, if you listen to Mexican Americans, we are the only ones who keep saying, "Oh yeah, I'm a 4th-generation, 5th-generation, 8th-generation American." We are continually reinforcing our right to be here because we are constantly being questioned about our right to be here. I hear many Americans saying "It doesn't bother that they stop me and ask me for my papers." But it doesn't happen to anybody else. It's a 4th amendment [of the Bill of Rights] violation to be stopped based on appearance.

There's a song, a very popular salsa song. The guy proposes to the girl. He says "Let's live together 'till the INS separates us." When I talk to agents, I say "That's how predominant you are in our lives. It's no longer until God do us part, it's until the INS do us part."

On career day here in Houston, talking with second and third graders . . . which are predominantly Spanish-speaking I tell them about the work I do. I ask "Do you know anything about the Border Patrol?" I've discovered nobody raises their hand. "How about La Patrolla Fronteriza?" Nobody raises their hand. I say "La Migra"and invariably out of a group of twenty about eleven will raise their hands and say that they've had experience with la Migra. They begin to tell me their family stories. When it happened to them at the bridge, at the checkpoint, to their mother and their father. Then I'll say "Any other stories?" Someone will always say, "We ran into one on the street the other day." Then I ask them "What color was the uniform?" "Oh it was blue." And I say, "No that's the Houston police department." What I tell the Border Patrol is "You are so predominant in our community that for these children the first uniformed authority that they learn to fear and learn to interact with is the INS or the Border Patrol. All other uniformed authorities extend from there." It's a predominant experience.

The Border Patrol destabilizes the community. Our own history tells us that if you raid a factory today, in a week, a week and a half, everybody's back. What does this do? The individual becomes unstable. The family unit is destabilized. The parents are gone, or the father is gone, whoever is gone, until they come back. You destabilize the community. You create a lot of instability. I think this is part of the mechanism of oppression.

"Disregard of U.S. migration law only causes problems for American citizens, especially those who immigrated here legally."

Illegal Immigration Creates Prejudice Against Legal Immigrants

Josh Moenning

In the following viewpoint, Josh Moenning makes a sharp distinction between legal and illegal immigration. America has a long tradition of immigration, he argues, and legal immigrants can both benefit themselves and enrich the nation. However, illegal immigration can lead to social problems such as crime and the formation of prejudices against minorities. The United States must take steps to control illegal immigration in part to ensure the future of legal immigration, he concludes. Moenning was an opinion columnist for the *Daily Nebraskan*, the student newspaper at the University of Nebraska.

As you read, consider the following questions:
1. Why would it be hypocritical to oppose all immigration, in Moenning's view?
2. What do polls reveal about America's public attitudes toward immigrants, according to the author?
3. What are some of the negative effects of illegal immigration, according to Moenning?

You have no idea how much it pains me to introduce a column with a President Bill Clinton quote. But I think that the president wasn't too far off the mark when he said, during his 1995 State of the Union address, "We are a nation of immigrants. But we are also a nation of laws.

"It is wrong and ultimately self-defeating for a nation of immigrants to permit the kind of abuse of our migration laws we have seen in recent years, and we must do more to stop it."

A Nation of Immigrants

We are undeniably a nation of immigrants. Many of us are the descendants of those tired, poor and huddled masses that came here to find the life they couldn't live in their native homelands. They came from every continent, every country and every land in search of a more fulfilling life.

Many came here relatively recently. Many of our ancestors, my own included, arrived in this country just a few generations ago.

With that said, it would be ridiculous for me to blame anyone for wanting to come here and start a new life today. It would be hypocritical of me to claim that the country that welcomed my great-grandparents years ago should today close its borders and disallow any influx of people wishing to better their lives.

However, it is necessary to acknowledge that our country does have a problem with immigration today. The problem is not with immigration itself. Legal immigration can create benefits for its participants and for the country as a whole.

Illegal Immigration

It is illegal immigration that causes problems and builds stereotypes. Disregard of U.S. migration law only causes problems for American citizens, especially those who immigrated here legally.

In order to deal with any problem, we must first know the extent of it. According to the U.S. Immigration and Naturalization Service, there were about 5 million undocumented immigrants residing in the United States as of October 1996. The population of undocumented immigrants was estimated to be growing by at least 275,000 each year. The two states with the largest number of illegal aliens were California, with an estimated 2 million, and Texas, with 700,000.

Legal Immigrants Are Unfairly Criticized

Increasing the number of Border Patrol agents, improving border barriers, and cracking down on document fraud are all forceful steps in the right direction. In addition, limiting the number of public benefits available to illegal aliens—while still allowing emergency medical care and school lunches for children—should help States reduce the now truly overwhelming costs of providing public benefits for illegal aliens.

But while I agree that illegal immigration is a problem that must be addressed by Congress, I am not convinced that our legal immigration program needs reform, and I am concerned that our hard-working legal immigrants have been unfairly criticized during debate on this issue.

Most immigrants come to this country in search of a better life for themselves and their families, not to receive a welfare check. The strong work ethic of immigrants has fueled American economic strength throughout our history and will continue to do so.

Nancy L. Johnson, *Congressional Digest*, May 1996.

In Texas, the state most directly in contact with the problems of illegal immigration, the general sentiment of citizens confirm the fact that illegal immigration has become a major problem and that more needs to be done about it.

A poll taken by the *Austin American-Statesman* in November 1997 showed that 82 percent of the 1,000 people surveyed considered illegal immigration a serious or very serious problem, and 61 percent said the federal government isn't doing enough to correct the problem.

Even when sorted by ethnic groups, the respondents who believed that illegal immigration is a serious problem in the state and in the rest of the country remained in the majority.

Eighty-six percent of non-Hispanic whites, 72 percent of blacks and 69 percent of Hispanics surveyed thought that illegal immigration had become a serious problem.

Now it isn't that the Texans surveyed believe that all immigration is a problem. The poll goes on to find that 71 percent of the respondents agreed that "there are positive benefits from legal or authorized immigration."

Separate Entities

What the Texans seem to realize, as should the rest of the nation, is that legal and illegal immigration are completely separate entities, and they should be viewed as such.

Immigration, when authorized and executed legally, can be a positive and beneficial experience for the immigrant and for all of America. The United States offers legal immigrants the land of opportunity, and legal immigrants offer the United States additional resources to the labor market. Immigrants often provide labor in jobs that many Americans refuse to take. Their help in these areas is necessary to keep many industries alive.

Illegal immigration, on the other hand, can lead to many negatives in society. One of the biggest of these is the formation of prejudices and stereotypes toward a dominant migrant group, like Hispanics in the United States. These stereotypes often carry over to negatively affect those immigrants who arrived in the country legally.

Illegal immigrants, simply by their residence in this country, show disregard for American laws. This disrespect for the law leads to another problem with illegal immigration, and that is the crimes that illegal aliens often commit while they reside here.

Overcrowded prisons are often a complaint in areas with a high level of illegal immigration. In addition, narcotics often find their way to this country across the border, smuggled in by aliens.

These problems, along with many others, were a major reason that the Illegal Immigration Reform and Responsibility Act passed in 1996. This act was designed to tighten controls on illegal immigration. It allows for significant additions to the border patrol, greater work-site enforcement and verification, increases in resources to combat alien smuggling and aids in the removal of deportable aliens.

It is a step in the right direction for effectively curbing illegal immigration in the future.

As the president said, we are undoubtedly a nation of immigrants. And it should be our responsibility, as a nation of immigrants, to ensure the right of others to legally migrate here in the future by successfully terminating the problem of illegal immigration today.

"There can be no successful control of illegal immigration without changes and reductions in its legal cousin."

The Problems of Legal and Illegal Immigration Are Inseparable

Mark Krikorian

Many Americans have expressed support for legal immigration while calling for more enforcement against illegal immigration. In the following viewpoint, Mark Krikorian argues that such an approach is flawed. Legal and illegal immigration are not two separate issues, he contends, but are instead part of the same process. America must lower the number of legal immigrants allowed to come here in order to curb illegal immigration, he concludes. Krikorian directs the Center for Immigration Studies, a research organization based in Washington, D.C.

As you read, consider the following questions:

1. What glaring omission exists in immigration legislation passed by Congress in 1996, according to Krikorian?
2. Why have the numbers of legal and illegal immigrants risen in tandem, as explained by the author?
3. How do long waiting periods for green cards contribute to the illegal immigration problem, according to Krikorian?

The Immigration and Naturalization Service (INS) recently reported that there were five million illegal aliens in the U.S. as of last fall [1996]—several hundred thousand more than the government had previously thought.

This marks a grim milestone. The number of illegals is now the same as it was before Congress passed the 1986 amnesty, which legalized nearly three million people. Clearly, the strategy of giving green cards to illegal aliens in combination with promises of stricter enforcement has failed completely.

Government efforts directed against illegal immigration have been woefully inadequate for a very long time. Congress and the administration have sought to rectify this over the past two years, culminating in last fall's immigration bill [the 1996 Illegal Immigration Reform and Immigrant Responsibility Act], which increased the Border Patrol, stiffened penalties on smugglers and document forgers and tightened up a wide variety of legal procedures.

A Glaring Omission

But a glaring omission guarantees that the illegal population will continue to grow: Congress and the administration emphasized that illegal immigration should be dealt with separately from legal immigration.

Proponents of this approach argue that the two are distinct; that one constitutes lawless behavior, while the other is a lawful process. This view results from a fundamental misunderstanding of how immigration works. In fact, legal and illegal immigration are merely two parts of the same process. And there can be no successful control of illegal immigration without changes and reductions in its legal cousin.

Why are they linked? Because the volume of legal immigration has risen together with illegal immigration. Legal immigration increased from 3.3 million in the 1960s to 7.3 million in the 1980s. At the same time, apprehensions of illegal immigrants by the Border Patrol increased from 1.6 million in the 1960s to 11.9 million in the 1980s.

It is no coincidence that legal and illegal immigration have risen in tandem. The communities of legal immigrants formed since the mid-60s serve as incubators for illegal immi-

gration by providing housing, jobs and entree for their com-
patriots who haven't yet managed to procure a green card.

Mexico is the No. 1 source of both legal and illegal immigrants. Other top sources of legal immigrants are, likewise,
senders of illegal immigrants.

Laundering Immigration Status

The evidence has become overwhelming that legal and illegal immigration are merely two sides of the same coin.
They've risen in tandem over the years, and most of the top
illegal-alien source countries are among the top sources of
legal immigration as well.

What's more, it's clear that legal and illegal immigrants are often the very same people, having used the "legal" immigration
system to launder their status. To cite just one piece of administrative evidence, the INS reported last year that between
1987 and 1996, about 1.3 million illegal aliens were given
green cards as part of the normal immigration process. In 1996
alone, 189,000 illegals were turned into legal immigrants.

Mark Krikorian, *Investor's Business Daily*, March 21, 2001.

In fact, illegal immigrants make up a significant proportion of major immigrant groups—they account for more than
one-third of all people in the U.S. born in Mexico, almost
half of Salvadorans and Guatemalans, nearly a third of
Haitians, 15 percent of Canadians, and 8 percent of Filipinos.

Long Waits

One of the dysfunctional elements of our legal immigration
policy that drives illegal immigration is the existence of
amazingly long waiting lists for green cards. There are more
than 3.5 million people who are qualified for immigration to
the U.S. but waiting their turn to receive the limited number of available visas.

The wait can be decades long—Filipino siblings of American citizens who are now receiving their visas have been
waiting almost 20 years; those applying today can expect to
wait as long as four decades.

Obviously, this suggests a seriously flawed mechanism.
And it encourages those who've been selected, but asked to
wait, simply to settle with their American relatives illegally.

The Commission on Immigration Reform headed by the late Barbara Jordan said such "extraordinary" backlogs "undermine the credibility of our policy" by encouraging those outside our borders to flout the rules.

The INS is now able to track how many of the people receiving green cards were already living here illegally. Astonishingly, more than one-fifth—22 percent—of legal immigrants were, in fact, illegal immigrants using the system to become legal.

This figure was more than triple what the INS expected. And an internal State Department survey has found that upwards of 90 percent of legal Mexican immigrants were illegal aliens.

Legal immigration clearly is a driving force behind illegal immigration—and cutting the former is a necessary prerequisite to gaining control over the latter.

Those working to demonstrate the need for comprehensive immigration reform obviously failed to make this clear during last year's debate [over 1996 legislation]. But with the illegal population nearing a record high—and with more than 400,000 illegals settling here every year—the debate won't end anytime soon.

Periodical Bibliography

The following articles have been selected to supplement the diverse views presented in this chapter. Addresses are provided for periodicals not indexed in the *Readers' Guide to Periodical Literature*, the *Alternative Press Index*, the *Social Sciences Index*, or the *Index to Legal Periodicals and Books*.

George M. Anderson	"Keeping Out the Immigrant," *America*, July 17, 1999.
Vernon M. Briggs Jr.	"Immigration Policy and the Plight of Unskilled Workers," *Social Contract*, Fall 1999.
Steven A. Camarota	"Does Immigration Harm the Poor?" *Public Interest*, Fall 1998.
Layne Cameron	"The Frontlines of Illegal Immigration," *American Legion*, March 2001.
Camile Colatosti	"The Flight into America," *The Witness*, December 1997.
Ken Ellingwood	"Study Tallies Cost of Illegal Immigration," *Los Angeles Times*, February 6, 2001.
Thomas J. Espenshade	"Unauthorized Immigration to the United States," *Annual Review of Sociology*, 1995.
Wade Graham	"Masters of the Game: How the U.S. Protects the Traffic in Cheap Mexican Labor," *Harper's Magazine*, July 1996.
Gene Koretz	"America's Secret Labor Force," *Business Week*, April 17, 2000.
Mark Krikorian	"Illegal Means a Lot," *National Review*, June 16, 1997.
Timothy W. Maier	"The People Smugglers," *Insight*, August 23, 1999.
Norman Matloff	"How Immigration Harms Minorities," *Public Interest*, Fall 1996.
Bill McKibben	"Immigrants Aren't the Problem. We Are," *New York Times*, March 9, 1998.
Mary Anastasia O'Grady	"Mr. President, Tear Down This Wall," *Wall Street Journal*, October 3, 1997.
Robert Park	"One Man's Border Battle: An Interview with Roger Barnett," *Social Contract*, Fall 2000.
John Parker	"Rising Illegal Immigration," *Traffic World*, August 14, 2000.

Marlene Peralta "Let My Friends Live Their American Dream," *New Youth Connections*, December 1998.

Peter H. Schuck "America Is Pro-Immigration After All," *New Republic*, April 13, 1998.

Richard Vedder, Lowell Gallaway, and Stephen Moore "The Immigration Problem: Then and Now," *Independent Review*, Winter 2000.

CHAPTER 2

Are Illegal Immigrants Being Victimized?

Chapter Preface

Few people would dispute that many illegal immigrants in the United States face harsh conditions and circumstances. For some immigrants, the trials begin with the journey to America. Between 1994 and 2000 more than fifteen hundred migrants died in the desert while attempting to enter the United States from Mexico. Those who survive and escape capture find themselves trying to build new lives with low-paying jobs, slum housing, and little legal recourse to fight against perceived injustices. In some cases, the conditions illegal immigrants live in approach slavery. In July 1999, Florida prosecutors won prison terms for six men convicted of luring Mexican women to the United States and forcing them to work off their smuggling fees in brothels. An August 1995 federal raid in Los Angeles revealed seventy illegal Thai immigrants who were confined behind barbed wire and forced to work in a garment sweatshop. Such instances are but an extreme example of the abuse, exploitation, and discrimination many illegal immigrants face, activists argue. "We have created a new, expendable, underclass of virtual slaves," concludes Julie A. Wortman, editor of the religious publication *The Witness.*

Yet to call illegal immigrants victims, some argue, is to miss a central point: Most immigrants chose to come to the United States, so in some sense the hardships they face are a matter of choice. Many do find better lives in the United States than those they left behind. In addition, critics argue that illegal immigrants simply are not entitled to the same rights and protections of U.S. citizens and legal immigrants. "Illegal aliens have no right to be treated like Americans" asserts educator James Coleman. "Unless they enter and remain legally, they have no right to our bounty." The viewpoints in the following chapter examine some of the burdens borne by illegal immigrants and their causes.

*"I do not believe that many American
citizens . . . really wanted to create such
immense human suffering . . . in the name
of battling illegal immigration."*

Targeting Illegal Immigrants for Deportation Is Unfair and Inhumane

Ann Carr

Some critics of U.S. immigration policy have called for a greater number of deportations. But Ann Carr in the following viewpoint argues that forcing illegal immigrants to leave the United States and return to their country of origin can have inhumane and unfair consequences. Carr, an attorney who practices in Pennsylvania, contends that laws passed by Congress making it easier to deport illegal immigrants (as well as legal immigrant residents convicted of crimes) have resulted in parents being separated from their children, the impoverishment of families, and other stories of human suffering. The American public, she believes, should be made aware of the hardships created by immigration policies.

As you read, consider the following questions:
1. What examples of hardship does Carr describe?
2. What do immigrants contribute to American society, according to the author?
3. In the author's view, why is flexibility in administering immigration laws important?

It is time the American public realized exactly what has been passed in their name.

One Family's Story

The young man fidgets as he sits across from me in the prison consulting room. As his immigration lawyer, I have just finished telling him that he is going to have to leave the country and go back to Mexico. The reason: He was guilty of the "crime" of working in the United States without permission, doing work that most Americans won't do, so that he could support his American wife and child. Earning one's living and supporting one's family used to be considered a virtue, last time I checked.

"But my wife is expecting her baby in a few weeks. How is she going to live if I can't work to support her?" His face quivers with the anxiety and stress this thought provokes. I am at a complete loss to explain to him the rationale of the law that mandates such a result—a young American family being deprived of the husband and father figure, and almost certainly being forced onto the welfare rolls to boot. The young man has fallen afoul of the recent legislation that sends people back to their country of origin to apply for an immigrant visa. They usually experience delays of a year or more before they can return. When he asks if there is anything he can do, I suggest that his wife, a U.S. citizen with a vote, call her Congressional representatives to ask them for a solution.

Harsh Laws

It is time the American public realized exactly what has been passed in their name and allegedly at the urging of the majority of the voting public. I do not believe that many American citizens (and maybe even many Congressional representatives) really wanted to create such immense human suffering, the separation of husbands and wives, parents and young children, the impoverishment of entire families, all in the name of battling illegal immigration. Think for a moment what it meant to a young mother to be deported recently, away from her six-month-old baby. There was no time to arrange for the baby to travel with her, and the father had to continue working to support the family, so she was sent back to Mexico alone. In desperation, she tried twice unsuccessfully to get back into the country to be with her child. On the third try, she died in the heat of New Mexico's desert. . . .

Family Traumas

The . . . deportation strategy has frightening implications for communities across the nation. Psychologists and social workers report that immigrants, particularly children, can be seriously traumatized by the experience of watching their family members and neighbors taken away. Pacific News Service described undocumented children hiding in the woods and refusing to attend school after a raid in Wimauma, Florida.

Sasha Khokha, "Criminalizing Immigrant Workers," National Network for Immigrant and Refugee Rights Fact Sheet, Spring 1997.

Why were such laws passed? Several recent studies have concluded that new immigrants contribute more to the economy overall than they take out, that immigrants do not commit proportionately more crimes than American citizens do, that immigrants in general come to the United States to work rather than to collect welfare, that immigrants perform the grunt jobs that Americans refuse to do, that immigrants bring energy and enterprise to a jaded society. These hard economic and sociological facts are true of both legal and illegal immigrants. If there were no Mexicans working in the fields, we would not have fruit and vegetables on our tables at affordable prices. Who else is going to spend 10 backbreaking hours a day picking strawberries, peaches, beans, tomatoes? Why is it seen as so antisocial to supply the labor for this need? For that matter, why is it so evil to migrate in search of a living? People have been doing it for thousands of years. It is part of the law of supply and demand, the free marketplace. Yet the Illegal Immigration and Immigrant Responsibility Act of 1996 creates impossible barriers and obstacles to the legal immigration of such people, many of whom have strong ties to family members who are American citizens or legal residents here. They are treated as though they are sub-human, with no right to live with their children or husbands or wives.

The act is at its harshest with regard to legal immigrants convicted of minor crimes in the past. Many may agree that non-citizens with serious criminal convictions should be returned to their country, especially if they show no signs of rehabilitation. But we are not just talking about serious crimes here. The expanded version of "aggravated felony" includes many crimes that are actually misdemeanors or even petty offenses, and the definition is applied retroactively. A legal resident with a second shoplifting offense from 1975 is now likely to be classified as an aggravated felon and find herself on the plane home with no possibility of forgiveness. A legal resident convicted of a simple assault in a pub brawl in 1980 could now be classified as an aggravated felon and lose everything—family, home, career. And this applies even if the person arrived in this country as a young baby with his entire family and doesn't speak the language of his home country. There is no flexibility, because changes in the law have removed all discretion in these matters from the U.S. Immigration and Naturalization Service and from the immigration courts. . . .

When I told a friend about what is going on, he said: "It seems so unnatural for Americans to kick people when they are down. These laws seem to have taken away from Americans the right to exercise their freedom to be humanitarian." And that is what has happened. Almost every element of flexibility and discretion has been removed from the current immigration laws. We are supposed to stop thinking of immigrants as human beings. Indeed, we are encouraged to see them as a plague on society, like so many rabbits to be rounded up and shipped out. We are being deprived of our freedom to show compassion; we are being deprived of our freedom to forgive. This is not only un-American, it is contrary to the moral principles of every great religion of the world. To quote from a prophet revered by two of these religions: "Only if you . . . no longer oppress the resident alien . . . will I remain with you in this place . . . which I gave your fathers long ago and forever" (Jeremiah 7:5–7). And we should not fall into the great and enduring mistake of thanking the Lord that we "are not as they are."

*"U.S. immigration laws . . . have become a
dead letter."*

The United States Should Deport More Illegal Immigrants

Joseph A. D'Agostino

One fundamental question in U.S. immigration policy is what to do with U.S. residents who illegally entered the country. In the following viewpoint, Joseph A. D'Agostino argues that illegal immigrants are largely ignored by the Immigration and Naturalization Service (INS) and other law enforcement agencies once they successfully enter the United States. Only a small fraction of illegal immigrants are ever deported to their country of origin. The result, he contends, is a rapidly growing population of illegal immigrants that has reached, by some estimates, eleven million people. D'Agostino is assistant editor of *Human Events*, a conservative weekly newspaper.

As you read, consider the following questions:
1. How big is the range between differing estimates on the illegal immigration problem, according to D'Agostino?
2. How many illegal immigrants does the author say were deported in 1999?
3. According to D'Agostino, when was the last major effort of the United States to remove illegal immigrants?

There may have been as many as 11 million illegal immigrants residing in the United States in 2001, according to a study by Northeastern University, but the federal government, charged by the Constitution with regulating immigration and defending the nation's borders, deported only about 1% of them.

The rest were allowed to stay and—if liberal Democrats have their way—may someday be given amnesty and allowed to become full-fledged U.S. citizens, and thus voters.

Seventeen Congressional Districts

They would equal the total population of 17 congressional districts and amount to about 20 times the difference in the popular vote in last November's presidential election [in 2000].

Following the 2000 Census, the U.S. Census Bureau originally estimated there were 6 million illegal immigrants in the country as of last year. But last month the bureau said it was revising that estimate, and might increase it to 9 million. Meanwhile, researchers at Northeastern University have released a report arguing that the real number of illegal immigrants residing in the U.S. is 11 million.

In fiscal 1999, the Immigration and Naturalization Service (INS) and other agencies intercepted at or near the border and deported approximately 1.6 million people trying to enter the country illegally or found ineligible for entry.

Failing to Enforce the Law

But once illegal aliens get past the border, enforcement of U.S. immigration laws virtually stops. In 1999, the INS managed to deport only 72,000 illegal aliens who were willing to leave voluntarily, and another 47,000, who left involuntarily after proceedings. That total, 119,000, is only about 1.08% of the total number of illegals that Northeastern estimated are now living in the United States.

Furthermore, according to the Census Bureau, each year about 400,000 new illegal immigrants sneak across our borders and settle permanently in the country.

U.S. immigration laws, in other words, have become a dead letter. They are completely meaningless—at least for people who are wealthy enough, or geographically close enough to the United States, to make it here without a legitimate visa.

Views on the INS

"Our Interior Enforcement units have limited resources," said an INS spokeswoman. "There are civil liberties issues involved in trying to identify illegal residents. Very often their employers protect them because they want inexpensive labor. But we have stepped up our targeting of employers since the 1996 immigration reform." She noted that the number of immigrants ruled inadmissible or found and deported, despite being minuscule in absolute terms, was a record for the period since 1965, when the current system of immigration laws was largely put in place.

Aliens Deported by Cause
Fiscal Years 1991–1996

Year	Total	Convictions for criminal or narcotics violations	Related to criminal or narcotics violations	Entered without inspection	Violation of non-immigrant status	Other
1991	28,923	15,538	476	10,919	974	1,016
1992	38,527	22,383	690	13,462	864	1,128
1993	37,238	25,188	409	10,395	536	710
1994	39,623	28,257	296	9,980	477	613
1995	41,819	29,145	247	11,390	433	604
1996	50,064	32,869	156	15,835	481	723

Statistical Yearbook of the Immigration and Naturalization Service, 1996, Immigration and Naturalization Service, U.S. Department of Justice, Washington, DC, 1997.

"The INS' budget has doubled in the last five years," countered a staffer for outgoing House Immigration Subcommittee Chairman Rep. Lamar Smith (R.-Tex.), who counts himself an illegal immigration hawk. "The INS has not been enforcing the law against illegal immigrants, especially the provisions in the 1996 bill that make worksite enforcement easier. We need an INS commissioner who will aggressively enforce the law at the border and everywhere else. . . . And as the congressman has said many times, President Bill Clinton's proposals for amnesties just encouraged more people to enter this country illegally."

Kent Wissinger, spokesman for incoming subcommittee Chairman Rep. George Gekas (R.-Pa.), said, "Congressman Gekas hasn't come to a conclusion on what needs to be done yet."

Past Efforts

It was over 45 years ago—from 1953 to 1955—that the INS conducted the last comprehensive push to root out illegal immigrants in the United States. "Some 2.1 million, mostly Mexican, illegal aliens were removed between 1953 and 1955," wrote David Simcox in a paper for the Center for Immigration Studies, which he chairs. "While abuses marred the effort, illegal immigration stayed under control for more than a decade."

The INS says that alien-smuggling is now an $8-billion-a-year industry and that smuggling rings are a top focus of its law enforcement efforts. "We believe this is a good way to target our limited resources and if we make it unprofitable for the smugglers, fewer people will come," said the INS official. She noted that the daily average detention population of the INS has grown to 20,000 detainees, up from 8,200 in 1997. "Our enforcement efforts have increased tremendously," she said.

Illegal aliens who reside in the country have the right to legal representation during deportation proceedings. The average case time has dropped since the 1996 reform and is now four years. The INS's budget doubled from 1995 to 1999, when it reached $4.3 billion.

Robert Bach, who served as executive associate INS commissioner under President Clinton, said, "If there is one idea that comes out of looking at these numbers it is, as we have said many, many times before, that over the past two decades or so the country has had insufficient resources and attention to the illegal immigration problem . . . and it has accumulated to where it is now a large and substantial issue."

*"Operation Gatekeeper'. . . has
accomplished little other than to create an
image of boundary control and to cause
large numbers of migrant deaths."*

The United States Is to Blame for Illegal Immigrant Fatalities

Joseph Nevins

In the following viewpoint, Joseph Nevins analyzes Operation Gatekeeper, an initiative begun in 1994 during the Clinton presidency by the U.S. Immigration and Naturalization Service (INS) to prevent illegal immigrants from crossing the Mexico-California border. He argues that the Border Patrol, given greater resources, has successfully discouraged illegal immigration into the city of San Diego, but the result has been an increase in illegal border crossings in remote mountain and desert areas. Nevins argues that the INS is thus at least partially responsible for the deaths of the migrants who have perished while attempting to enter the United States. Furthermore, he contends, Operation Gatekeeper has had the effect of discouraging resident illegal immigrants from returning to Mexico. The United States must develop more productive and humane approaches to illegal immigration than militarizing the border, Nevins concludes.

As you read, consider the following questions:
1. What was the goal of Operation Gatekeeper, according to Nevins?
2. According to the author, how many would-be immigrants have perished since Operation Gatekeeper began?

From "How High Must Operation Gatekeeper's Death Count Go?" by Joseph Nevins, *Los Angeles Times*, November 19, 2000. Copyright © 2000 by Tribune Media Services. Reprinted with permission.

On Oct. 1, 1994, the Clinton administration launched "Operation Gatekeeper," the enhanced border enforcement strategy of the U.S. Immigration and Naturalization Service (INS) in Southern California. Six years later, it is clear that the expensive operation has accomplished little other than to create an image of boundary control and to cause large numbers of migrant deaths. Such reasons alone should lead us to put an end to the fatally flawed strategy. More important, however, the failure of Gatekeeper should force us to question our whole approach to unauthorized immigration and national boundaries in a world where social relations increasingly transcend such boundaries.

The administration began Gatekeeper with much fanfare. It was a time of persistent economic downturn and a historically unprecedented level of public and political activism in favor of cracking down on illegal immigration. In some ways, it was the administration's response to the pressure from increasingly restrictionist Republicans in Congress, but especially that of then-California Gov. Pete Wilson and the feared passage of Proposition 187 [a proposal to deny public education and other public services to illegal immigrants].

In other ways, it was the administration's answer to the massive disruption in Mexico's rural and small business sectors brought about by growing economic liberalization, a process greatly intensified by the North American Free Trade Agreement (NAFTA). It was for this reason that INS Commissioner Doris Meissner argued to Congress in November 1993 that responding to the likely short-to medium-term impacts of NAFTA "will require strengthening our enforcement efforts along the border, both at and between ports of entry."

As the centerpiece of the Clinton administration's Southwest border enforcement strategy, Gatekeeper provided the INS in Southern California with unprecedented levels of personnel, technology and infrastructure. The number of agents in the Border Patrol's San Diego sector, for example, has grown from 980 in 1994 to more than 2,200. As a result of such changes, it is undoubtedly more difficult to cross the border now. Gatekeeper has pushed migrants from urban areas into more unforgiving and risky terrain and forced them to rely on high-priced smugglers. Indeed, the ultimate goal of the new enforcement strategy is to make it so difficult and costly to enter the United States extralegally that fewer people try to do so.

Consequences of Operation Gatekeeper

But research at UC San Diego indicates that, overall, Gatekeeper is having little effect in stemming unsanctioned immigration to California. Migrants have learned to adapt and are utilizing increasingly sophisticated and expensive smugglers to evade the Border Patrol. In this regard, Gatekeeper has had an unintended consequence: Once in, the immigrants are now less likely to migrate back to Mexico in the off-season and are staying in California for longer periods of time.

Perhaps the greatest accomplishment of Gatekeeper has been to make undocumented immigrants less visible and thus give the appearance of a border under control. Meanwhile, growing numbers of migrants perish beyond the media spotlight in the mountains and deserts of California's border region.

By the Border Patrol's own criteria, such an outcome suggests that Gatekeeper is somewhat failing. The Border Patrol and INS officials expected that Gatekeeper would discourage a significant number of migrants from crossing by pushing them out into mountain and desert areas where, after making a cost-benefit analysis, they would rationally decide to forgo the risks and return to Mexico. Given that this is not happening, the INS is arguably partially responsible for the deaths. By knowingly "forcing" people to cross such terrain, the INS has contributed to the resulting deaths.

But the INS refuses to acknowledge any responsibility, instead blaming smugglers for leading people into high-risk areas and positioning itself as the defender of the migrants. In June 1998, for example, the INS launched "Operation Lifesaver," involving civil patrol flights to spot migrants in distress and increased search and rescue missions in hazardous areas. As Claudia Smith of the California Rural Legal Assistance Foundation contends: "As long as the strategy is to maximize the dangers by moving the migrant foot traf-

Operation Gatekeeper, the border-enforcement strategy implemented in 1994, is a failure. Here's what we taxpayers have paid for: double the number of border agents since 1994, a large number of portable and stationary stadium-type lights; extensive fencing, new road construction, motion detectors, infrared night scopes, and a computerized system called IDENT to help the Border Patrol identify repeat offenders. Yet even more people are crossing the border—only in different places or by different means. The failure of this strategy has resulted in the deaths of hundreds of people in the last six years. This strategy has increased the numbers of smugglers and their links to crime. Because it is too dangerous and too costly to return home, immigrants are obliged to stay on this side of the border; Gatekeeper has created a permanent buildup of immigrants on the United States side of the border.

Since the inception of Operation Gatekeeper in 1994 at least 600 people have died trying to cross the border between San Diego, California, and Yuma, Arizona. The death toll for 2000 is 140.

Susan Luzzaro, *North County Reader*, February 22, 2001.

fic out of the urban areas and into the mountains and deserts east of San Diego, the deaths will keep multiplying."

Hundreds of Deaths

One such death was that of 20-year-old Jose Luis Uriostegua. Border Patrol agents discovered his frigid body on Mount Laguna in eastern San Diego County, about 20 miles north of the U.S.-Mexico boundary, this past March 22, 2000. He has been designated No. 500—the 500th person to perish while trying to evade the U.S. Border Patrol in Southern California since Gatekeeper began. The count is now [as of November 2000] up to 603.

Fleeing from Guerrero, one of Mexico's poorest states where human rights abuses are rife, Uriostegua was struggling for a better life for himself and his family. Rather than seeing the world as divided, he saw it as whole. In this respect, the young man recognized what many of our political imaginations do not allow us to see: The U.S.-Mexico boundary, as a line of control and division, is an illusion.

Mexico and California are increasingly one.

On a more practical level, moreover, a law enforcement approach to immigration is destined to fail. The ties between the United States and Mexico are too strong, migrants are too resourceful and Americans are too resistant to the police-state measures that would prove necessary to significantly reduce unauthorized immigration.

Rather than try to create new and improved methods to repel those who cross our borders—but whose hard work we welcome—we should embrace them. At the same time, we need to appreciate that immigration is often the result of the breakdown of political, economic and social systems and work with various sectors of Mexican society to redress such phenomena. This would prove to be a far more humane and effective method for addressing the myriad factors that lead people to migrate than continuing what sociologist Timothy Dunn appropriately describes as the "militarization" of the border.

Had Uriostegua made it to Los Angeles, he might be mowing your lawn, busing your table or picking your tomatoes. He would be one of the hundreds of thousands of unauthorized immigrants who form the backbone of California's booming economy. Immigrants are human beings who, regardless of their legal status, deserve our respect and solidarity, not poverty wages or a potential death sentence.

Mexico's president-elect, Vicente Fox, already has shown himself to be open to rethinking the nature of the U.S.-Mexico boundary. This provides people on both sides of the international divide with an opportunity to move beyond immoral, ineffective and ultimately counterproductive approaches to the complexities of immigration that inextricably bind our two countries.

"Mexico's refusal even to try to stop the exodus of its own population ought to tell us that it has no concern . . . with the welfare of its own people."

Mexico Is to Blame for Illegal Immigrant Fatalities

Samuel Francis

In recent years hundreds of migrants from Mexico have died while attempting to cross into the United States. Some observers have blamed the United States and its border security efforts for driving would-be illegal immigrants into more dangerous areas. In the following viewpoint, Samuel Francis argues that the migrants themselves are to blame for violating U.S. laws, and Mexico shares culpability for failing to discourage illegal immigration to the United States. Francis is a syndicated columnist.

As you read, consider the following questions:
1. How many illegal immigrants does the author say are arrested in San Diego?
2. What remarks by Mexican official Fernando Solis Camara does Francis object to?
3. What does Mexico's actions regarding migration reveal about Mexico, according to Francis?

L ike hurricanes and sex in the Oval Office, illegal immigration is something that everybody is still against. Yet—again like hurricanes and presidential sex—illegal immigration keeps happening. In 1998, despite vastly improved border security on the American side, arrests of illegals in San Diego alone are expected to exceed 200,000. But while almost all American politicians support tougher controls, their Mexican counterparts are openly refusing to take any measures to reduce the flow.

In September 1998, the *New York Times* reported that the head of Mexico's migration service simply refuses to do anything to discourage his fellow countrymen from violating U.S. laws and international agreements by moving north. "At no time will we take any action that could discourage Mexicans from emigrating to the United States," pronounced the official, Fernando Solis Camara. "That is because these are people who leave their families and their homes with the legitimate goal of bettering their lives."

Mexico's Callousness

His remarks betray a good deal about the Mexican government and its aims that Americans, politicians or not, need to think about. In the first place, it tells us that Mexico actually wants its own population to invade the United States—partly to get rid of what it considers excess people, partly because it regards (at least unofficially) the southwestern United States as still Mexican, and partly because, as Mexican leaders have openly stated in the past, Mexicans in this country can build a fifth column that the compadres in Mexico City can manipulate to their advantage.

But Mexico's refusal to staunch its own demographic overflow tells us something else as well: The Mexican government really doesn't much care about its own people or their welfare. Mr. Solis's remark was uttered in the context of a relatively new dispute over border security. As U.S. border security improves, illegals are driven away from the areas where they used to enter this country into more remote and more dangerous areas, with the result that more and more of them are being discovered—dead.

In California alone, more than 90 Mexican immigrants

have been found dead in 1998. They get lost in the desert and die of thirst and exposure. Or they put their trust in smugglers, who simply abandon them as soon as they rake off their money. A new agreement between Mexico and the United States requires each country to place signs that are supposed to warn immigrants against trying to cross the border in certain areas. The United States has in fact placed more than 100 such signs.

Yet champions of unrestricted immigration in this country whine that the immigrant deaths are all the fault of the United States. If we hadn't increased security at the borders, they argue, then not so many immigrants would try crossing in dangerous places and fewer would die. That argument, of course, ignores the reality that the immigrants are violating our laws. If they don't want to die or risk death, maybe they should stay home.

Immigration and the Mexican Government

Americans ought to be sick and tired of the Mexican government pushing its problems off on us. It is the Mexican government's responsibility to create an economy in which its people can make a decent living and live a decent life. Instead, the government exploits the hell out of them and sends them across the border to earn money to send back to their families in Mexico.

Charley Reese, *Social Contract*, Fall 2000.

And if the Mexican government gave a plugged peso for the well being of its own people, it would fire Mr. Solis and seriously try to discourage its own people from coming. Doing so might even help improve relations with the United States, whose people would then not be acquiring the sneaking suspicion that the Mexicans think most gringos in the Southwest ought to pack up and go back to Plymouth Rock.

But the Mexican government not only does not fire Mr. Solis; it backs him up. The Mexican consul general in Los Angeles tells the *Times* that the Mexican Constitution gives Mexicans the right to move where they want, and that includes other peoples' countries. Besides, he beams, "Here in the U.S., there also are laws that give the Border Patrol the responsibility to prevent people without documents from entering the country."

It's nice the consul general acknowledges the right of the U.S. government to do that, but of course we couldn't expect a little cooperation from him or his government, could we? As long as we can't, and as long as Mexico openly refuses to take any measures to stop the flow of illegals, the United States is perfectly justified in solving the problem the most effective way it can.

Mexico's refusal even to try to stop the exodus of its own population ought to tell us that it has no concern whatsoever either with the welfare of its own people or with respecting the laws and interests of its northern neighbor. As long as that's the case, our government should stop pretending that our neighbor to the south is a friend or an ally and start considering whether it may be an enemy whose real purpose is simply to conquer our land by tolerating, if not actually encouraging, its occupation.

"[Immigrants] put up with injuries, chemicals, and below-poverty-level wages because other jobs are closed to them."

Illegal Immigrants Are Victimized by Unscrupulous Employers

Jane Slaughter

Jane Slaughter is a labor writer based in Detroit, Michigan. In the viewpoint that follows, she tells of how immigrant workers, many of them illegal, are being exploited by employers who pay them low wages and subject them to unsafe working conditions. She holds that many employers purposely use undocumented workers because they are more willing to accept dangerous and low-paying jobs. Government laws against hiring illegal immigrants are seldom enforced and are easily circumvented by forged documents, she contends.

As you read, consider the following questions:

1. Why are illegal immigrants more willing to take jobs other people do not want, as explained by Slaughter?
2. What industries and lines of work does the author contend have become dominated by immigrant labor?
3. What role have unions played for illegal immigrants, according to Slaughter?

At a 1997 rally in Wenatchee, Wash., apple warehouse worker Roberto Guerrero told the story of how he came from Mexico to the U.S. He traveled, he told the crowd, with several other Mexicans stacked between sheets of plywood in the back of a truck. He and his undocumented associates joked to each other, said Guerrero, that if they died on the way, at least they were already in their coffins.

Now a citizen, Guerrero is trying to convince his employer, Stemilt, Inc., to recognize the union that a majority of his fellow workers say they need. They want a living wage and a way to protest unsafe conditions.

"I feel so sad how they treat my people," says Guerrero, speaking of his co-workers. They come, like him, from Mexico, or from El Salvador, Guatemala or Cambodia. They sort, store, and pack a billion dollars worth of apples each year. Roberto himself works in the "seg room," where it's always 30–35 degrees, segregating different sizes and qualities of apples and pears, stacking heavy boxes of fruit.

"It's like the Indians a long time ago," he says. "They [the employers] give little things, and my people give them the gold."

Targeting Immigrant Workers

The "gold" nowadays, of course, is cheap labor. Entire industries—garment, electronics, meatpacking, agribusiness— maintain their profit margins by specifically targeting immigrant workers as their employees. Immigrants take the low-paying, dangerous jobs that others don't want.

They run great risks to come to the U.S.—such as traveling in "coffins"—because the abysmal pay they get here is still better than what they could find in their home countries. Once they are here, they put up with injuries, chemicals, and below-poverty-level wages because other jobs are closed to them. Better jobs are beyond reach because of lack of skills, language problems, and, in the case of undocumented workers, fear of discovery.

Certain American industries thrive on that fear.

"Food processing in America today would collapse were it not for immigrant labor," says Mark Grey of the University of Northern Iowa. Grey has studied the systematic recruitment by Midwestern beef, pork, and poultry packers of Laotian and Latino immigrants, both legal and undocumented.

Meatpacking is the most dangerous industry in the country. In recent years one after another well-paying, unionized meatpacking plant—employing white, native-born workers—has shut down. They have reopened in smaller towns, offering $6 an hour to a new type of workforce. In Storm Lake, Iowa, for example, Iowa Beef Processors proffered $150 bounties to Laotians who recruited relatives to come to work there. The majority of the workforce is now composed of immigrants. Turnover is 80 percent each year.

Similarly, electronics and garment factories deliberately set up in areas of high immigration: Los Angeles, Silicon Valley, New York City. Seventy-seven percent of the lowest-paid jobs in Silicon Valley's computer industry are held by immigrant workers, with employers now preferring Asian women, perceived as more "docile" than Latinas. Half the industrial workers in Los Angeles are Latinos; 87 percent of the apparel workers there are Latinos or Asians.

"Manufacturing in Los Angeles depends on immigrant workers," concludes union organizer Peter Olney. In some major cities, the janitorial workforce—those who clean the big downtown buildings by night—is now mostly Latino immigrants, and the migrant workforce that picks tomatoes, cucumbers, and citrus fruit is essentially all Latino immigrants and their children.

Circumventing Sanctions

It's been 11 years since Congress [in 1986] enacted sanctions on employers who hire "illegal" immigrants, touted by conservatives at the time as a means to stop the influx of foreigners. All employers are now required to verify a new-hire's citizenship status, and employers caught with undocumented workers on the payroll may be fined. In practice, these "sanctions" have done nothing to discourage potential immigrants. They are easy to circumvent, as documents are easily counterfeited. And they are seldom enforced. Employers calculate that the cheap labor is worth the risk of a fine. In New York City, for example, the U.S. Immigration and Naturalization Service (INS) collected less than $5,000 in employer fines in 1996—even though that year saw a big increase in INS raids on workplaces.

Far from deterring employers from hiring immigrants, the sanctions have actually, in effect, encouraged them to do so. When an employer sees signs of organizing among his immigrant employees, he can threaten to call the INS on himself. This ensures an intimidated workforce.

"With the help of the INS," wrote Sasha Khokha of the National Network for Immigrant and Refugee Rights, "employers can police their workforce at will using the only armed force in the country specifically designed to regulate labor."

The INS plans to double the number of its agents over the next five years. But, as one undocumented worker from Mexico told *The Nation*, "Everyone knows they are never going to arrest all of us. Who would do this shitty work for them? We know that every now and then the *migra* will come in and take a few away to keep the politicians happy. That's how it works."

Poor Pay, Dangerous Work

This "shitty work" may pay below the minimum wage, for women toiling at home sewing machines or in Chinatown sweatshops in New York or San Francisco. A well-publicized government raid in 1995 on an El Monte, Calif., garment sweatshop turned up 70 Thai immigrants being held in slave-like conditions. They were forbidden to leave their combined working and living quarters, surrounded by razor wire, till they had paid off the cost of their passage to America. One woman had been held for seven years. California State Labor Commissioner Victoria Bradshaw, who led the raid on the sweatshop, professed astonishment at the conditions.

When 209 undocumented meatpackers were arrested in Iowa in 1996, their average pay was found to be $6.02 an hour, or $12,521 for the few who manage to work an entire year. The nature of the work—wielding knives on animal carcasses—makes them highly susceptible to repetitive strain injuries, as well as wounds. If they are injured, they are unlikely to get compensation, both because of lack of knowledge of how to work the system, in the case of legal residents, and because of fear of discovery, in the case of illegal ones.

When the janitorial workforce was transformed in the 1980s from native-born to immigrant, wages fell. In Los Angeles, for example, pay dropped from nearly $10 an hour in 1977 to just over $6 in 1993 (in 1993 dollars). In Silicon Valley, electronics assemblers earn the lowest wages of any occupation other than food preparation. The solvents and solders they use, often with no gloves, can cause loss of smell and memory, scarring of the lungs or cancer, according to the Santa Clara Center for Occupational Safety and Health.

Toxins are part of the worklife of migrant strawberry pickers, too. In 1996 the California legislature delayed a planned prohibition of deadly methyl bromide, used to kill parasites. And in 1994 the Environmental Protection Agency reduced the amount of time employers must wait before sending workers into fields treated with the fungicide captan, a known carcinogenic. Workers are receiving up to 200 times acceptable doses, says a labor/environmental coalition.

Strawberry workers' average wage is $6.29 an hour, usually from piecework—a 20 percent drop from 20 years ago. Some, the most recent immigrants, sleep in the fields. Workers have sued one company for forcing them to do calisthenics before work and pack berries at the end of the day without pay.

Garment shops use the piecework system, too. Chinese immigrants at Lucky Sewing Co. in Oakland found that a dress for which they were paid $4 to $5 retailed for $175 under the Jessica McClintock label.

The irony of such low wages is that they prevent workers from obtaining legal status for their families. The law says that the person petitioning on behalf of family members must make 125 percent of the federal poverty level. For a family of four, the petitioner would have to earn $20,062 per year. The average full-time wage for an apple warehouse worker is $12,000; half that for a picker in the orchards.

An "Explosion" of Union Organizing

Given the isolation, the language barriers, and the legal problems, it's remarkable that some of the most exciting—and successful—union organizing in the country is happening among immigrant workers. Janitors, farm workers, drywallers, tortilla delivery drivers, food processors—the 1990s have seen a virtual explosion of militant struggles, including strikes and civil disobedience.

Best known are the 40,000 janitors who've joined the Service Employees union over the last 10 years. The union's Justice for Janitors (JfJ) campaign avoids the stacked-deck procedures of the National Labor Relations Board and uses marches and community support to pressure owners of big office buildings. In the Century City area of Los Angeles, for example, Central American janitors wearing red bandannas and union T-shirts invaded the swanky watering holes frequented by yuppie executives during happy hour. Their strike won them a contract. JfJ is now organizing in Sacramento, suburban Philadelphia, Washington, D.C. and suburban Denver.

The union is using a second pressure tactic: asking large stockholders to use their influence with janitors' recalcitrant employers. The Episcopal Church Pension Fund is one such large stockholder. After prodding by 80 bishops, Fund managers have agreed to meet with representatives of janitors seeking a union contract in Washington, D.C.

Midwestern migrant farm workers, through their union the Farm Labor organizing Committee (FLOC), have done away with the archaic sharecropping system on tomato farms. Through both their own organizing and a large dose of church support, they forced the large tomato-buying corporations—Campbell, Heinz—to sign three-way agreements with the union and small family farmers. Now FLOC is targeting cucumber workers in North Carolina. Last year, 150 tortilla drivers in Los Angeles won a 46-day strike and a 24 percent pay increase. Three years earlier, disgusted with arbitrary firings and no pay for overtime, they had begun meeting in secret. They went looking for a union, and found Teamsters Local 63.

"Unions aren't really targeting the immigrant community," says Joel Ochoa, who works for a Teamster-backed organizing center. "Immigrant workers are organizing themselves, and going to unions for assistance."

"Ecclesiastes Says the Union Is Good"

The apple warehouses of central Washington are yet another battleground. A majority of workers at two key companies have signed with the Teamsters, but owners have fired key leaders and refused to recognize the union. At the same time, the organizing has already had a positive effect, with the company giving a 35-cent wage increase, a week's vacation, and a Christmas party. The union has a monthly radio show in Spanish. They've enlisted religious leaders to lead rallies and speak from the pulpit. In August 1997, workers marched on their employers to demand a contract, setting up a "bargaining table" and folding chairs outside company headquarters.

Roberto Guerrero was one of them. He and his wife Carmen have five kids. He makes $8.41 an hour now—but he's among the higher paid workers because he's been on the job for eight years.—they get a 10-cent raise each year.

An ardent Pentecostal Christian, Guerrero's pro-union

rap is sprinkled with allusions to God's will. "Ecclesiastes says the union is good, you know," he contends.

"Chapter 4, verse 9 says two are better than one; because they have a good reward for their labor. And verse 12, it says, 'If one prevail against him, two shall withstand him; and a three-fold cord is not quickly broken.'

"That is the union. If I go in front of the boss, he fires me, but if we go with 20 or 40 or 50 guys together, he don't fire us so easy."

"The most important abuses . . . [of immigrant workers] are the result of government."

Illegal Immigrants Are Victimized by Misguided Government Policies

Wendy McElroy

Wendy McElroy is a contributing editor to *Ideas on Liberty*, a publication that promotes economic freedom and individual rights. In the following viewpoint, she argues that while some illegal immigrants are exploited in sweatshops and other hazardous workplaces, many immigrant advocates are mistaken in their belief that more government regulation is the solution. She argues that it is government policies and their enforcement—especially federal laws against hiring illegal immigrants—that are the primary cause of the excessive exploitation of immigrant workers. She contends that employers will pay appropriate wages for labor (which would be low for the unskilled labor that many immigrants perform) and that immigrant workers could collectively unionize and bargain to improve their position if the labor market is kept free from government interference.

As you read, consider the following questions:
1. What actions by the Immigration and Naturalization Service (INS) have, in McElroy's contention, affected immigrant workers?
2. What would be the effect of laws against sweatshops, in the author's view?

The nineteenth-century phenomenon of sweatshops is re-emerging as an important 21st-century issue for American labor and business. For example, the United Students Against Sweatshops has called on its 180 campus affiliates to organize and force universities to deal only with manufacturers who abide by fair labor practices. In February 2000, students from the University of Pennsylvania staged a much publicized sit-in in front of the president's office to ensure that the logo apparel sold by the university was not produced by sweatshop labor.

Although the students admitted that they had no evidence that any apparel had been produced by sweatshops, they thought it was "a safe assumption." The university agreed to withdraw from the Fair Labor Association, which students called "an industry-controlled monitoring system that only serves to cover up sweatshop abuses" and "a public-relations operation designed to improve the image of its members, like Kathie Lee Gifford and Nike." Instead, the university agreed to join the Worker Rights Consortium—a human rights and labor organization that advocates the "rights" to a living wage and to unionize in the Third World. But labor activists quickly point out that sweatshops exist in America too. Indeed, they seem to be a growing trend. A "Garment Enforcement Report" (April–June 1999) from the U.S. Labor Department reported that 205 sweatshop investigations resulted in the discovery of 109 violations.

In the Austin *American-Statesman* (February 27, 2000), journalist Martha Irvine offers a typical account. Irvine begins by focusing on the harsh labor conditions of a tortilla factory on Chicago's South Side, then goes on to report the wider findings of the Center for Impact Research. "More than a third of the 800 workers questioned—many of them immigrants—described conditions in factories, restaurants and other workplaces that the federal government would deem sweatshops." As a result of this report and ensuing publicity, the U.S. Department of Labor announced its intention to work with ethnic community groups in order to uncover abusive employers.

This is a common pattern in anti-sweatshop activism— stories of personal exploitation are coupled with thin statistical analysis, which collectively result in a superficial governmental response. Often, the abuse is real. Sometimes, it is hideous. Unscrupulous employers are always blamed—and with cause. Government is always the proposed solution, with disastrous results.

Why Sweatshops Exist

Few people seem to question one of the fundamental reasons that nineteenth-century sweatshop conditions exist in 21st-century America. Free-market advocates correctly point out that low wages are appropriate to untrained, unskilled workers and that many of the sweatshop conditions are no more than what naturally occur in the lowest-paid strata of employment. But, arguably, the most important abuses—for example, an inability of employees to organize or to enforce agreements—are the result of government. In this the Immigration and Naturalization Service (INS) must bear particular responsibility. As one of the tortilla factory workers explained to Irvine, "Because they [laborers] don't have papers, the bosses think they can do what they want." Employees who are not authorized by government to work have little or no protection against employers who break contracts and coerce their labor through threats. Usually they threaten to turn employees or their undocumented family members in to the INS for deportation.

Papers proving a worker's eligibility for employment became mandatory in the United States under the Immigration Reform Control Act (IRCA) of 1986. IRCA requires employers to complete an I-9 Form for "new hires" in order to record the documents that establish the worker's employment eligibility. Immediately, undocumented workers became vulnerable to abuse. For example, if an undocumented employee protests a breach of contract, he (or members of his family) can be reported to the INS.

The relationship between undocumented workers and the big labor unions is more complicated. In 1986, the AFL-CIO vigorously backed IRCA, largely because it gives American workers an extreme advantage in the labor market. For over a decade, Big Labor watched contentedly as every employer—under threat of legal sanctions—filled out an I-9 form on every employee. Now powerful unions such as UNITE (Union of Needletrades, Industrial and Textile Employees) call for the repeal of those sanctions. AFL-CIO Secretary Treasurer Richard Trumka declares, "we are all illegals . . . in the eyes of Wall St." By this statement he links the interests of American laborers with those of undocumented immigrants, both of whom are the alleged victims of exploitative capitalism. Thus Big Labor demands additional regulation to prevent sweatshops. The regulations being demanded are designed to solve problems that the unions themselves helped to create through their former support of INS policies. To understand Big Labor's shift on undocumented workers, it is necessary to sketch some history.

Abuse Created by the INS

Requiring I-9 forms on every new worker soon became inadequate for the government to "protect" American labor. In 1998 the agency grew tired of needing grounds for suspicion to conduct background checks on specific types of employees. Thus began an experiment called "Operation Vanguard"—a fishing expedition within the meatpacking industry of the midwest. The INS subpoenaed the employment records of all meatpacking plants in Nebraska, then cross-referenced them against Social Security and other government databases to determine which workers had proper employment authorization. After the initial industry-wide audit, the INS followed up with additional audits at regular intervals to check on new hires. (The program has since been extended to other states, with the INS proposing to hire private firms to run the relevant background checks. Such firms would not be subject to the same restraints as governmental agencies.)

When a discrepancy appeared in a document, the worker in question was ordered to appear at an INS interview. In many, if not most, cases the discrepancy was the fault of the INS. "The information on these databases is notoriously bad," explains Josh Bernstein, senior policy analyst at the National Immigration Law Center. "And because the database is flawed, a lot of people who have employment authorization end up showing up as illegal."

Even if they are legal, many foreign workers decide to quit their jobs rather than be interviewed by the INS. "It's like an IRS audit, except imagine that you face the threat of going out in handcuffs," Bernstein says. Further, many legal workers leave their jobs because a family member is not documented, and so they don't want to undergo an interview.

INS Raids Harm Communities

Since the passage of employer sanctions regulations, numerous studies have documented a climate of heightened discrimination, fear, and hostility against immigrant workers—or anyone who "appears" to be foreign. Instead of deterring immigrants from working, mandates for documentation verification and Immigration and Naturalization Service (INS) raids have been utilized as tactics to perpetuate an abusive working environment and push the immigrant economy even further underground. Employers hiring undocumented workers are able to extract long working hours for low wages because they know that workers without papers are usually workers without access to a formalized grievance process. Even more insidiously, employers frequently call the INS "on themselves" if they suspect that employees may be preparing to engage in collective action or strategies for unionization.

Sasha Khokha, "Criminalizing Immigrant Workers," National Network for Immigrant and Refugee Rights Fact Sheet, Spring 1997.

Horror stories of INS abuses as well as negative memories of government in their home countries mean that many workers simply flee. Usually, they are forced to work off the books at less attractive jobs where they have no seniority and where the employer may know how much they fear the INS. For example, on May 5, 1999, INS agents arrived at an IBP meatpacking plant in Lexington, Nebraska, to question more than 2,000 workers. The INS had previously reviewed the plant's I-9s and had found 318 discrepancies. On the date of the interviews, however, 185 of the workers under suspicion had left. Of the remaining 133, one was arrested and one was fired. The INS sweep disrupted plant operations and terrorized hundreds of workers.

One INS tactic in particular is almost a formula for creating sweatshops. As a general part of its strategy, the INS has encouraged employers to become partners in the government's verification process. Employers are urged to use an electronic employment program called "Basic Pilot," a joint project of the INS and Social Security that lets employers check up on all employees by accessing government databases. Basic Pilot was first used in California, Florida, Illinois, New York, and Texas, but has been expanded.

Offering employers access to government databases is part of an INS strategy called "interior enforcement"—that is, the enforcement of immigration law away from the border. In the eyes of already fearful immigrant workers, the employer is now an arm of the INS. Indeed, workers-rights groups warn that the INS is using employers as enforcement agents. Of course, having incriminating information on an employee gives an employer a great negotiating advantage. Some unethical employers have exploited this advantage to the detriment of undocumented workers who no longer feel able to enforce contracts or complain of abuses. Workers who participate in a union can be reported to the INS. In essence, the INS has given employers a green light to create sweatshops.

Big Labor on Undocumented Workers

At its 1999 annual convention in Los Angeles, top officials of the AFL-CIO admitted having made a mistake in backing the IRCA. But the government harassment of immigrant workers is not what provoked Big Labor into changing its stance. After all, such compassion had not prompted the AFL-CIO to advocate the protection of immigrant labor in the past. Rather, Big Labor's concerns were twofold: First, union membership has been declining across the board for decades. In the 1950s, 35 percent of U.S. workers belonged to a union. Today, the percentage is close to 14. To hold steady at that level, unions have to recruit 400,000 workers a year. With union figures stating that one in ten workers is foreign-born, Big Labor has come to a tardy conclusion: immigrant labor needs unions. . . .

The second reason for Big Labor's shift on IRCA is the upsurge in union-busting that has accompanied this measure. Especially in the area of agriculture, farm managers have called on the INS repeatedly to pick up undocumented workers who were key figures in union drives. For example, nearly 1,700 employees were fired from 13 apple-packing houses in the Yakima Valley of Washington state in March 1999. These businesses had been the targets of intense organizing by the Teamsters. By sweeping the apple-packing houses clean of workers with "discrepancies," employers also destroyed the rank-and-file leadership of the growing union. Arturo Rodriguez, president of the United Farm Workers, claims that Bear Creek Production Company, a California rose grower, arranged to have 15 percent of the union's members fired through an INS review of documents. "These are workers that have been here 15, 20, 25 years," he states, "have houses, have families, are in the educational system, have paid taxes, are members of their communities. They asked them to demonstrate their status in this country. And then they were evicted and lost their jobs."

Some employers have been more subtle. For example, when employees at a garment factory in California joined UNITE, foreign-born union members were called into the office and required to produce their documents over and over again for verification. Other workers picked up the clue. Union support declined dramatically. Ironically, the largest barrier to the AFL-CIO's recruitment of immigrant members and the organizing of new unions is the very law it championed in 1986—IRCA. No wonder labor councils and local unions across the nation are beginning to call for repeal of those aspects of the measure that make it illegal for an undocumented worker to hold a job.

Government Monitoring Is Not the Answer

Despite this cautionary lesson on how government regulation and monitoring of business harms workers, one of the remedies for sweatshops being sought by unions is more government regulation and monitoring. For example, UNITE applauded the February 7, 2000 announcement of New York City Council Speaker Peter Vallone concerning an anti-sweatshop bill he is sponsoring. The bill would prohibit the city from purchasing apparel—including uniforms for policemen—from manufacturers who do not disclose their locations and allow inspections. In some ways, Big Labor is manifesting the same knee-jerk response that Kathie Lee Gifford did on discovering that her Wal-Mart clothing line was being produced by sweat labor. Gifford went on a crusade to impose more laws on business. When New York Governor George Pataki signed path-breaking anti-sweatshop legislation in 1996, he stated, "In no small measure, this bill is going to be signed this afternoon because Kathie Lee Gifford and Frank Gifford made this a personal crusade." The legislation holds liable manufacturers and retailers who knowingly purchase, ship, or deliver goods produced by sweatshops. Such legislation will do nothing more than drive labor practices further underground where abuse can flourish unseen.

In the end, it will be the marketplace—not legislation—that determines the value of labor and the working conditions laborers will accept. The prevailing economy provides an opportunity for unions if they are willing to work with and not against market forces. Unemployment is extremely low, especially in the unattractive jobs, such as sewing, meatpacking, and agriculture, to which immigrant workers tend to gravitate. What workers need right now, while their negotiating position is strong, is the ability to bargain honestly and above-board for better wages and working conditions. Government can only interfere in this process.

Periodical Bibliography

The following articles have been selected to supplement the diverse views presented in this chapter. Addresses are provided for periodicals not indexed in the *Readers' Guide to Periodical Literature*, the *Alternative Press Index*, the *Social Sciences Index*, or the *Index to Legal Periodicals and Books*.

T. Alexander Aleinikoff	"Illegal Employers," *American Prospect*, December 4, 2000.
George M. Anderson	"Punishing the Immigrant," *America*, February 19, 2001.
David Bacon	"Labor and Immigrant Workers," *Z Magazine*, October 2000.
Anthony Depalma	"Farmers Caught in Conflict Over Illegal Migrant Workers," *New York Times*, October 3, 2000.
Ken Ellingwood	"Border Agents Take on Role of Lifesavers," *Los Angeles Times*, August 29, 2000.
Kenneth Hamblin	"Bordering on the Unacceptable," *Conservative Chronicle*, June 18, 1997.
Chris Hedges	"Spousal Deportation, Family Ruin," *New York Times*, January 10, 2001.
Rick Henderson	"The INS Is Cracking Down on Illegal Workers, But It's Still Very Easy to Come Up with Phony Papers," *Los Angeles Business Journal*, December 1999.
Matthew Jardine	"Operation Gatekeeper," *Peace Review*, September 1998.
Rosemary Johnston	"Mourning Deaths of Migrants," *National Catholic Reporter*, April 27, 2001.
Siu Hin Lee and Celeste Mitchell	"Sweat Shop Workers Struggle in New York's Chinatown," *Z Magazine*, October 1998.
Carol Nagengast	"Militarizing the Border Patrol," *NACLA Report on the Americas*," November/December 1998.
Debbie Nathan	"Border Geography and Vigilantes, *NACLA Report on the Americas*," September 2000.
William G. Paul	"America's Harsh and Unjust Immigration Laws," *USA Today*, July 2000.
Revolutionary Worker	"The War on Immigrants and the Resistance in Arizona," October 15, 2000.
Margot Roosevelt et al.	"Illegal But Fighting for Rights," *Time*, January 22, 2001.
Alan Zarembo	"Coyote Inc.," *Newsweek*, August 30, 1999.

CHAPTER 3

How Should America Respond to Immigration?

Chapter Preface

In 1986, America had an estimated population of three to five million illegal immigrants. That year, as part of the most sweeping change in immigration law in thirty-four years, Congress took the controversial step of reducing the number of illegal immigrants by legalizing them. Under Section 245A of the Immigration Reform and Control Act (IRCA), illegal aliens who had resided in the United States since before 1982 could apply for temporary or permanent residence. Approximately three million applications for legalization were processed by the Immigration and Naturalization Service (INS) within the next several years; 88 percent were admitted as permanent legal residents.

Amnesty (legal forgiveness) for illegal immigrants was criticized when it was first enacted, and whether to extend it to more recently-arrived immigrants is a source of debate to this day. The fundamental objection, as John Tanton argued before a Senate committee in 1981, was that amnesty for people who had come to the United States illegally made it "a reward for that illegal act" and would encourage more illegal immigration. But proponents of amnesty argue that it is a better alternative than imprisoning, deporting, or ignoring America's illegal immigrant population. "Undocumented immigrants are part of the fabric of . . . [American] communities," asserts Catherine Tactaquin, director of the National Network for Immigrant and Refugee Rights. "We would all stand to gain from legislation that brings the undocumented from out of the shadows." As these statements suggest, the debate over amnesty, like many concerning illegal immigrants, hinges on whether to punish illegal immigrants as criminals or attempt to integrate them as members of the U.S. community. Amnesty is one of several controversial policy alternatives towards illegal immigrants that are examined in this chapter.

"One look at the ravages of illegal immigration in California is enough to make most Americans sick."

America Must Take Stronger Measures to Halt Illegal Immigration

Michael Scott

Michael Scott is a businessman from Southern California, an area that is home to many illegal immigrants. In the following viewpoint, he argues that the American government is not doing enough to enforce immigration laws and stop what he calls a "relentless flood" of illegal immigration. Among the steps he recommends is to deport illegal immigrants, increase border enforcement, and prosecute employers who hire illegal immigrants. Failing to control illegal immigration will result in great harm to the United States, he concludes.

As you read, consider the following questions:
1. Why are Americans hesitant to propose strong action against illegal immigrants, according to Scott?
2. What two basic actions does the author recommend to eliminate illegal immigration?
3. What does Scott consider to be the biggest lie of all?

In 1991, I accidentally stumbled upon a botched illegal immigration operation on a nearby Southern California beach—in broad daylight. Nearly one-hundred illegal immigrants were hiding in a few tiny gullies, partially protected by a cadre of lookouts, presumably waiting for transportation to get them to their destinations. Neither the local police nor Los Angeles Immigration and Naturalization Service (INS) showed much concern. This resulted in my researching the background and realities of illegal immigration, and the more I learned, the worse it got. We've got a ticking time bomb on our hands, made worse by legions of government officials who just slumber on, or push their heads deeper into the sand to curry favor with those who support this relentless invasion. Just as bad, lots of Americans have been sucker-punched into inaction by threats of being called "racist", "bigot" and sundry yada yada.

Then, in 1999, I had a conversation with Arizona rancher Roger Barnett, whose property is under year-round siege by hordes of illegal aliens. His Chochise County border sector is overwhelmed by about 475,000 illegal aliens annually. Although Barnett has apprehended over 1000 illegal aliens on his property and turned them over to the Border Patrol, he's anything but a vigilante. Roger has lived in Douglas, Arizona all of his 50-some years, and is infuriated by the on-going destruction of his property caused by incessant swarms of illegal immigrants, as well as by the repeated failures of the INS to stem this relentless flood. Barnett and his neighbors have had it with an unmerciful stealth migration that generates mountains of rotting garbage, piles of discarded diapers, food containers and plastic water bottles, and sundry filth everywhere—exacerbated by the stench of excrement, poisoned (or throat-slit) pets and livestock, torn down fences, and lots of stolen property that wasn't tied-down.

Of special ire is Barnett's 80-year-old widowed neighbor who lives behind her chain-link fence, with a shotgun and pistol always near by, and who's afraid to come out at night and challenge the hoards who have ruined her crops and garden, and made her a virtual prisoner in her own home. She's afraid to buy more guard dogs since the last two were poisoned, probably by "coyotes" [immigrant smugglers].

Costs of Illegal Immigration

One look at the ravages of illegal immigration in California is enough to make most Americans sick. At least 40 percent of the nation's 6 million illegal immigrants are here. From a base of 2.4 million illegal immigrants already present, they just keep coming—120,000 net new illegals each year into California (300,000 nationally), and the horrendous social costs just keep rising. There are 408,000 illegal immigrant K-12 students to educate at a cost to California taxpayers of approximately $2.2 billion annually, for example. Never mind that these students can't work, drive or vote once they graduate, unless they obtain fraudulent documents.

Taxpayers subsidize 96,000 illegal immigrant births in statewide county hospitals (200,000 nationally) at a yearly cost of $352 million. Then we have annual . . . [welfare] costs for these new citizen children of nearly $552 million. Add another $557 million to incarcerate 23,000 illegal alien felons in California, plus $60 million health care costs for various services, and we're over $3.7 billion annually—out of our pockets, and against our overwhelming opposition to such outrages.

Eliminating this brutal migratory devastation involves two basic actions, enforcing our own immigration laws, and accepting the ugly reality that "we've met the enemy and it is us".

Enforcing the Law

Three fundamental law enforcement steps must be taken to break the back of illegal immigration. First, our borders must be sealed. No more baloney about how difficult this might be. The INS instituted a Border Patrol crackdown in 1994 in the El Paso sector, and then took it to San Diego a year later. In 1993, 90 percent of all illegal aliens crossed at border cities. Today [in 2000], two-thirds cross in remote areas. In 1994 in the San Diego sector, 42 percent of all illegals surged through a 14 mile corridor near Imperial Beach. Another 22.6 percent entered in and around El Paso. Both sectors are now almost impregnable, as these flows have become trickles. So today's illegals are going where it's easier to get across, like Douglas, Arizona. The inescapable conclusion is that the crackdown has succeeded where sufficient resources have been applied. This isn't a matter of insufficient resources or wherewithal, it's a matter of insufficient willpower, as well as a writing-off of those individuals and organizations who want illegal immigration to succeed.

The next critical law enforcement step is to prosecute employers who hire illegal aliens. The Justice Department is hardly lifting a finger in this area. If there were no jobs, most illegal aliens would leave, or most wouldn't come in the first place. The fantasy of illegal immigration cheerleaders that the economy would collapse without illegal labor simply doesn't wash. Since when don't we enforce laws (or break them) in accordance with our own standards of right and wrong? I sometimes speed on California interstates, and I'm prepared for the fines if caught. But this doesn't excuse me from punishment, nor the California Highway Patrol (CHP) from enforcement.

This baloney about the need for "guest workers" is pure bunk. Both the California Division of Labor and the General Accounting Office (GAO) have confirmed there are currently two farm workers for every agricultural job in California. This glut of farm workers has depressed agricultural wages over the past twenty years, in inflation adjusted terms, by 20 percent, and spawned deplorable working conditions. Job opportunities for low-skilled workers have been declining for three decades. The continued influx of low-skilled, uneducated immigrants has depressed earnings and limited opportunities. Income disparity has widened as a result of too many low-skilled workers pursuing too few jobs.

A University of California (Davis) agricultural economist (and several other noted researchers) published "Poverty Amid Prosperity," a compilation of research findings on "The processes of immigration and its unexamined impacts on cities and towns." (July 1997; The Urban Institute Press) They offered the following analysis (on pp. 89-90) of the impact of farm worker wage increases on both grower expenses and the price of food:

> And suppose that the entire cost of higher farm wages is passed on to consumers, so that the annual cost of the farm labor used to produce the fresh fruit consumed by the average American household rises from $8.60 to $13 and the cost of farm labor rises from $10.20 to $15. If these increased farm labor costs were completely passed on to consumers, spending on fresh fruits and vegetables eaten at home for a typical 2.6 person consumer unit would increase by less than $10, from $270 to almost $280.

I'd welcome the opportunity to pay higher consumer prices to rid our land of illegal immigrants. We'd lift an enormous financial albatross from our backs, and provide better educational opportunities for thousands of American kids to receive the full attention of teachers in schools crowded with the children of illegal immigrants.

Americans Willing to Work

Finally, to address perhaps the biggest lie of all—that Americans won't do the work that illegals perform, the truth is that uneducated and unskilled Americans won't live in garages with multiple families, and endure similar hardships to take on backbreaking work at below minimum wages. Get rid of illegal immigrants and wages would have to rise to attract those native-born and legal residents who lack the skills and education to do much else.

About deportation. With the exception of illegal alien felons incarcerated in various prisons, and those illegals caught by the border patrol, (at the border) deportations are virtually nonexistent. Yet there are six million illegal aliens in this country. We could make a huge deportation dent in this stealth population if we only had the commitment and determination to do so. Once again, it's a national administration attempting to curry favor with the wrong people.

About, "we've met the enemy and they are us," some conservatives and liberals support Cardinal Roger Mahony's statement, "the right to immigrate is more fundamental than that of nations to control their borders"—conservatives because they get their jollies from exploiting cheap labor, and liberals because it gives them another opportunity to smother someone with compassion. Added to these afflictions are the wishes of politicians to get reelected by ducking issues, and the hidden agendas of opportunists and ideologues to advance their causes. . . .

Proposition 187

Let's look at California's Proposition 187. This was a 1994 ballot initiative that barred illegal immigrant access to public social services, including education and public health care services, except emergency care. In November of 1994, 59 percent of the California electorate voted for Proposition 187. Of California's 58 counties, 49 voted yes.

The day after Proposition 187 passed, a federal court in Los Angeles, and a state court in San Francisco barred enforcement of most of its provisions. A federal judge kept this bottled-up for nearly 3½ years before voiding it. Immediately thereafter the State of California appealed the decision, but because a conniving governor was soon thereafter elected—a person opposed to Proposition 187—he saw to it that the initiative never reached the Supreme Court through the appellate process.

Just before Governor Gray Davis strangled Proposition 187 in April 1999, he said with the most angelic of faces, "If this (Proposition 187) were a piece of legislation, I would veto it. But it's not. It's an initiative, passed by nearly 60 percent of the voters through a process specifically designed to go over the heads of the legislature and the governor. If officials choose to selectively enforce only the laws they like, our system of justice will not long endure." Davis then walked off the press conference stage and betrayed the people of California by stabbing them in the back. . . .

Our Own Worst Enemies

Then there's the shameful AFL-CIO [labor union] clamor for amnesty for 6 million illegal aliens, hoping lots of them will become union members. The AFL-CIO is attempting to line their pockets with membership dues over the short run, while rolling the dice with the futures of American workers. All this will do is end control of our borders and unleash terrible wage depression pressures on millions of American workers as hordes of foreigners surge across unprotected borders looking for American jobs.

We've clearly become our own worst enemies and will suffer a terrible fate unless we end this madness. A series of national administrations have buried their collective heads in the sand and ignored the acrid odors of the white hot burning fuse attached to the illegal immigration time bomb. There just aren't enough Roger Barnett's around, and that's what's necessary for us to retake our country. Just remember folks, the only card your opponents hold in their hands is the race-baiting card, the threat of calling you a racist or a bigot. But the collective votes of an ignored and aggrieved articulate voting population are the strongest cards of all, and if you chose to play them, it's a slam-dunk for the good guys.

Illegal immigration is repudiated by our laws, by the facts, and by most Americans. So, one more time folks, let's seal our borders, deport all illegal aliens, prosecute any employer hiring illegals, throw the rascals out who live on the Planet Beltway and kowtow to the illegal immigration lobby, and begin to pay close attention to the calamity that awaits us unless we do all of these things.

"Acting on immigration as if it were a national crisis is today both unsustainable and undesirable for states under the rule of law."

America Must Cooperate with Other Nations in Regulating Immigration

Saskia Sassen

Saskia Sassen is a sociology professor at the University of Chicago and the author of several books on migration and globalization, including *Guests and Aliens* and *Globalization and Its Discontents.* In the following viewpoint, she contends that while the United States and other wealthy nations often view immigration from poorer countries as a national crisis that requires strong police action, such a unilateral approach is counterproductive in today's globalized economy in which goods, money, and people routinely cross national borders. In addition, attempts to stop immigration through military or police activities threaten the civil rights of immigrants and the general rule of law. She argues that the United States should work with other countries in formulating new policies to manage, rather than stamp out, immigration.

As you read, consider the following questions:

1. How does growing awareness and the constitutionalization of civil rights in the United States affect immigration law enforcement, according to Sassen?
2. According to Sassen, what three factors explain why militarizing borders is not the best solution for regulating immigration?

From "Immigration Policy in a Global Economy," by Saskia Sassen, *UNESCO Courier*, November 1998. Copyright © 1998 by *UNESCO Courier*.

Immigration is increasingly seen in terms of threats. The prevalent image of this threat in the developed countries of the North is one of mass invasion by hundreds of millions of poor from around the world. The overarching response in these countries is to militarize their borders and to maximize policing inside them. Immigration thus becomes suffused in a mentality of national crisis, and unilateral sovereign action emerges as the only effective response.

A Changing Context

This is of course not the first time in the history of the twentieth century that immigration has been portrayed as threatening and that there has been a clamour for strong unilateral state action. But today [1998] the context has radically changed. States have been forced by major economic trends to approach more and more matters multilaterally. Unilateral strongman tactics in military operations are less acceptable in international fora and are generally seen as less effective than multilateral approaches. For the first time innovations in international law have subjected national states to supranational authorities.

The context is also radically different when it comes to the use of policing as a key approach to more effective immigrant regulation. Today far more civil rights instruments are available to judges and there is a growing trend towards the constitutionalizing of civil rights in both the United States and in Europe. There are also far more human rights instruments available to judges and they are much more likely to be used than was the case even ten years ago.

Finally, there is a sharpening sense of the concept of civil society. Strategic sectors of the citizenry, especially in the United States, have asserted their right to criticize and even take to court various government agencies, most particularly police agencies. These conditions contrast sharply with the call for stronger police action vis à vis immigrants. When the object of stronger police action is a broad spectrum of people—immigrant women, men and children—sooner or later it will get caught in the expanding web of civil and human rights, it will violate those rights and interfere with the functioning of civil society.

In the United States, for example, the Immigration and Naturalization Service (INS) can now excercise its police authority on individuals merely suspected of being unauthorized immigrants. If my son decided to go write the great American novel by spending time with farm workers or in garment sweatshops, and there was an INS raid, he could well be one of the suspects, because I know he would not be carrying his US passport with him. Many of these INS actions can escape accountability in front of a judge if the persecuted are merely suspected of being undocumented. Sooner or later stronger policing and the weakening of judicial review of such police actions will interfere with the aspiration towards the rule of law that is such a deep part of our inheritance and our lived reality. Sooner or later, this type of police action will touch us, the documented.

Defending the Rule of Law

Acting on immigration as if it were a national crisis is today both unsustainable and undesirable for states under the rule of law. Precarious and partial as the concept of the rule of law may be, and imperfect as its implementation is, it is nonetheless an impressive tool in the struggle for a better and more democratic society. Aspiration to it strongly conditions political and civic order in the highly developed countries. The rule of law in good part means the right of citizens to be free from abuses by the state and is not enhanced by the expanded use of policing as an instrument to maintain control over immigration.

Since it is likely that cross-border migration will continue as the world becomes increasingly globalized, it is urgent that we rethink and innovate on the policy front. As we develop the cross-border integration of markets for goods and services, for capital, for information, and for communications, I would argue that the flow of people will continue apace. This will be especially the case among the top level professionals whose mobility is an essential part of the integration of markets, and among low-wage workers for whom cross-border mobility is often the only option.

The powerful actors in the new economic order, such as global corporations and global markets often more powerful than many a government, are already hard at work setting up, albeit a mostly private, system of rule that protects the rights of these actors no matter what country they choose for their operations. And states, many enormously reluctant, have joined in the multiplying multilateral efforts that the new economic order demands. More and more of them have relinquished capacities and competences, and even bits and pieces of their sovereignty, in the name of a more effective multilateral economic order. They have done so not only de facto, in some low-level, close-to-the-ground operational sense, but also de jure through the formalization of these changes in national and international law. Yet in the realm of immigration policy we see the continuation, and even strengthening, of unilateral state action, the invocation of absolute and undiminished state sovereignty.

This raises several questions concerning the viability, effectiveness and desirability of such a framework for policy. Can such an immigration regime be viable when most other cross-border flows are increasingly centered in multilateralism and diminished state sovereignty? Even if it is viable is it the most effective way of proceeding? Similarly with the expansion of a policing approach. Is it viable or effective in the context of a strengthening civil society and human rights? When it comes to desirability, the issues around immigration are probably more ambiguous than in the case of trade and capital flows, and become entangled in a variety of well-founded rationales along with ill-guided political passions.

I believe that multilateralism is a better way to proceed in a broad range of matters, including immigration, because it is essential to create—and invent—policies that have receiving and sending countries working together. I also consider the expansion of policing undesirable and not the way for enlightened societies to proceed. Whatever the control achieved, the trade-offs are too costly both for the immigrants themselves but also especially for the receiving societies in terms of violations of civil and human rights and the threats to the fabric of civil society.

Regulation is necessary but achieving it does not necessitate militarizing borders and maximizing internal policing. Why? Because of a combination of three factors. First, far from being a mass invasion, immigration is patterned and bounded in time and space. Second, national states are acquiring greater competence in multilateral management because of economic globalization and hence may be more competent to develop multilateral co-operation mechanisms with sending countries. Third, again because of economic globalization national states have had to learn to accommodate a growing number of conditions and norms coming from international fora. This combination of factors signals the possibility of new approaches to regulating immigration.

The Costs of Declaring War on Immigrants

Declaring war on illegal immigration is a good applause line, but wars, lest we forget, impose terrible sacrifices. Such bellicose rhetoric reflects and reinforces an alarmism that does more harm than good. Unintended but predictable border incidents, vigilantism, racially motivated violence, and discrimination in the workplace are the types of consequences that ethnically diverse societies can ill-afford—and all rich countries are now ethnically diverse.

Furthermore, such rhetoric effectively precludes a rational assessment of various policy options. The actions it inspires—militarizing borders, requiring national I.D. cards, or conducting highly intrusive workplace raids and indiscriminate street sweeps—sully a state's standing in the international community and raise serious concerns about civil liberties. Witness the huge outcry in Mexico each time the United States ups the enforcement ante on its southern border, or in civil rights and ethnic communities when enforcement actions mistakenly violate the rights of legal immigrants and citizens. Perhaps even more damaging in the long run may be that such extremism conveys the message to less developed countries that overreacting in matters of unwanted immigration should be tolerated.

Demetrios G. Papademetriou, *Foreign Policy*, Winter 1997–1998.

The key to a more enlightened and less crisis-oriented approach is the fact that migrations are patterned. The evidence about international migrations in the United States, in Western Europe and in Japan shows that international migrations are patterned, bounded in scale and duration, and conditioned by other processes. They are not simply an indiscriminate flow from poverty to prosperity as is suggested by the imagery of "mass invasions". If poverty were enough to produce emigration, then the developed countries would indeed be threatened with massive invasions. But it is only a very tiny fraction of all the poor who emigrate and they do so from very specific areas and towards equally specific destinations.

Furthermore, most migrations end. They do not go on for centuries. Fifty years seems to be a fairly lengthy duration for most cross-border migrations in the United States and Western Europe—that is to say, specific migration processes of a given nationality group to a particular location. Indeed, twenty years is probably more common in Europe. One of the reasons for this is that such migrations tend to be embedded in the cycles and phases of the receiving areas. Dramatic examples of this include the migrations of hundreds of thousands of Italian and Spanish workers to northern Europe that were in full swing in the 1960s and basically ended in the 1970s. Today, when Italians and Spaniards are free to move within Europe, there is almost no new migration. That particular phase of labour migration, embedded as it was in the post-war reconstruction of Europe and then in the expansion of the 1960s, came to an end when these conditions no longer held, and Spain and Italy became prosperous.

If international migrations are conditioned, patterned and bounded processes, the policy response need not be confined to maximizing border control. We can move away from a mentality of national crisis to one of management. This may be a good time for such a change. There is some consensus about the existence of a widening gap between immigration policy intent and immigration reality in the major developed receiving countries. An important nine-country study published in 1994 [Wayne A. Cornelius et al, *Controlling Immigration. A Global Perspective*, 1994.] found that the gap between the goals of national immigration policy (laws, regulations, executive actions, etc.) and the actual results is wide and growing wider in all major industrialized countries. It also found that immigration officials in all nine countries were less confident about the effectiveness of policy than their predecessors fifteen years before.

Rethinking Immigration

Major changes in policy approaches are a complex matter. Certainly the implementation of a new economic order required an enormous amount of problem solving and innovation. It is not evident to me that the last round of negotiations on the General Agreement on Tariffs and Trade (GATT), the so-called Uruguay Round, was any less complex than immigration regulation. It took years of work, but it got done. I am convinced that we need a radical rethinking of key aspects of the regulation of immigration and an enormous amount of innovation if we are to have a more effective and enlightened set of immigration policies. Some of this work is under way in the European Union, which has seen considerable and at times radical innovations in the last ten years on the subject of immigration.

Finally, there is now a so-called "concerted consensus" among a growing number of national states around the shared objective of furthering economic globalization and the major policy orientations that come with it—deregulation, privatization, anti-inflation policies, and foreign-exchange parity with the leading currencies. These are all fundamental conditions for the implementation of global capital markets. Along with the World Trade Organization and the environmental agenda, they have forced states to develop new competences to act multilaterally. They may suggest that national states can be led—or forced—to adopt a more international understanding of subjects such as immigration that used to be regarded in purely domestic terms.

*"Our current immigration policy
perpetuates a black market in immigration
[and] leads to workplace exploitation."*

Resident Illegal Immigrants Should Be Given Amnesty

Miguel Perez

In 1986 Congress passed the Immigration Reform and Control Act that, among other things, granted amnesty to illegal immigrants who could demonstrate continual residence in the United States prior to 1982. Approximately 2.7 million people took advantage of the law to gain legal status. However, the number of illegal immigrants residing in the United States has continued to grow since then due to continued migration. Various proposals for granting amnesty to more recent immigrants continue to be raised. In the following viewpoint, newspaper columnist Miguel Perez argues in favor of a bill introduced in February 2001 by Luis Gutierrez, a Democratic member of Congress, that would grant amnesty to most of America's illegal immigrants. Perez argues that since illegal immigrants play an important role in America's economy and pay taxes, they deserve legal residency in the United States.

As you read, consider the following questions:

1. Who supports amnesty for illegal immigrants, according to Perez?
2. What questions must amnesty supporters be prepared to answer, according to the author?
3. According to Perez, why are many Republicans opposed to amnesty?

I believe in it. I really do. If it was up to me, a new bill introduced in Congress by Rep. Luis Gutierrez, D-Ill., would be the law of land as of tomorrow. But is it realistic? Nah!

Gutierrez wants to give amnesty to practically every illegal immigrant in the country—the same country where the GOP (Republican Party) majority in Congress recently refused to be "compassionate" with much smaller groups of immigrants who are trying to adjust their status here. The Gutierrez bill would cover some six million [resident illegal immigrants].

Yet a blanket amnesty for illegal immigrants is now endorsed by many Congressional Democrats, labor unions, immigrant-rights organizations, and the president of Mexico.

Arguments for Amnesty

They say that illegal immigrants keep our economy going, that immigrant agricultural laborers feed this country and the world, that many of our factories and restaurants would shut down if we didn't have these people working here. They argue that our current immigration policy perpetuates a black market in immigration, leads to workplace exploitation, undermines enforcement efforts, and has people dying while trying to enter the country.

They say the Gutierrez bill is realistic because it acknowledges that these illegal immigrants are part of the fabric of America.

The Gutierrez bill would grant amnesty and offer legal residency to any illegal immigrant who has been in the country since 1996, and allow those who entered the country through Feb. 6, 2001, to apply for amnesty in the next five years.

Gutierrez said illegal immigrants make up half of the agriculture work force, pay a billion dollars in taxes in New York, and are a vital part of Washington's $1.2 billion fruit industry.

"Who in this country doesn't recognize when they eat grapes, who picked those grapes? Who in this country doesn't recognize when they eat an orange, who picked those oranges?" Gutierrez asked.

Heavy Opposition

But Gutierrez and his supporters are not being realistic if they don't recognize that this ambitious and controversial bill faces heavy opposition from those who say such a policy will only fuel more illegal immigration.

What do they say to those who will remind us that since the last amnesty law in 1986, which gave green cards to three million people, the number of illegal immigrants has doubled?

Don't tell me that amnesty makes a lot of sense, because I agree. You are preaching to the converted. The question is how do they convince those who control Congress and the White House that amnesty may be a good way to show they are truly compassionate?

The AFL-CIO Calls for Amnesty

Millions of hard-working people who make enormous contributions to their communities and workplace are denied basic human rights because of their undocumented status. Many of these men and women are the parents of children who are birthright U.S. citizens. The AFL-CIO supports a new amnesty program that would allow these members of local communities to adjust their status to permanent resident and become eligible for naturalization. The AFL-CIO also calls on the Immigration and Naturalization Service to address the shameful delays facing those seeking to adjust their status as a result of the Immigration Reform and Control Act.

Immediate steps should include legalization for three distinct groups of established residents: 1) approximately half-a-million Salvadorans, Guatemalans, Hondurans, and Haitians, who fled civil war and civil strife during the 1980s and early 1990s and were unfairly denied refugee status, and have lived under various forms of temporary legal status; 2) approximately 350,000 long-resident immigrants who were unfairly denied legalization due to illegal behavior by the INS during the amnesty program enacted in the late 1980s; and 3) approximately 10,000 Liberians who fled their homeland's brutal civil war and have lived in the United States for years under temporary legal status.

Policy statement of the Executive Council of the American Federation of Labor-Congress of Industrial Organizations (AFL-CIO), February 16, 2000.

What do they say to those who argue that amnesty rewards illegal immigrants without solving the problem of illegal immigration in the future, that it sends a message that you can come to this country illegally, because eventually you'll get your green card? What kind of a message does amnesty send to people around the world who are waiting for legal visas to come to the United States?

Unless amnesty proponents promise to find a way to shut down illegal immigration in the future, how can they expect the new Congress to be more compassionate than the last one?

Scare Tactics

Let's face it: Part of the Republican constituency are American xenophobes who falsely associate illegal immigrants with crime, disease, and loss of national identity. These are people who think that immigrants come to collect welfare, refuse to learn English, and have little education—when there is ample evidence to the contrary.

In the past, many Republicans have even used scare tactics to gain votes. And in spite of the party's much-promoted courtship with Latinos recently, many of them are not yet willing to part with their xenophobic constituency, especially when some politicians even had a part in creating it.

Even President George W. Bush, the champion of compassionate conservatism, "does not think that amnesty is the best way to approach this problem," said a senior administration official in a White House briefing a day before Bush went to Mexico [in February 2001) to meet President Vincente Fox.

Former President Bill Clinton had threatened to veto a major spending bill unless amnesty legislation for a much smaller group of immigrants was approved. But in the end Clinton caved in and the immigrants got only a small fraction of the legislation they had been seeking.

Which leads me to believe that has to be Gutierrez's strategy with his ambitious bill: Ask for a lot so you can get a little, because if you ask for a little you get crumbs.

4

"*Extending a blanket amnesty tells inhabitants of the impoverished Third World that if they can sneak past the Border Patrol, Uncle Softie will eventually welcome them with open arms.*"

Illegal Immigrants Should Not Be Given Amnesty

Don Feder

In the following viewpoint, Don Feder, a conservative syndicated columnist, argues against granting amnesty to illegal immigrants. He argues that passing a blanket amnesty that legalizes the status of illegal aliens would reward those who break the law and encourage more illegal immigration to this country. Moreover, it would be unfair to those who go through the process of legal immigration. Illegal immigration creates crime, welfare, and other social problems, and should be restricted, Feder contends.

As you read, consider the following questions:
1. What do most Americans associate with illegal immigration, according to Feder?
2. What were the characteristics of immigrants given amnesty in the 1980s, according to the author?
3. How does Feder characterize the Democrat and Republican positions on illegal immigration?

From "Amnesty Is Open Door to Illegal Aliens," by Don Feder, *Boston Herald*, February 14, 2001. Copyright © 2001 by the Creators Syndicate. Reprinted by permission of Don Feder and Creators Syndicate, Inc.

Rep. Luis Gutierrez (D-Ill.) thinks illegal immigration is great for America. Philanthropist that he is, the congressman wants to give us more of a good thing.

Gutierrez has filed legislation to allow virtually every illegal alien in the country (an estimated 5 million) to stay. Those who arrived before Feb. 6, 1996, would immediately qualify for a green card [Permanent Resident Card indicating lawful resident status]. Those who came between that date and Feb. 6, 2001, could apply for legal residency after five years.

"People in this country know they are benefiting from the work of undocumented workers," Gutierrez argues. "Why not grant them the dignity and justice that comes with permanent legal residency?" Dignity and justice are euphemisms for government benefits and the ability to bring in their relatives.

A Gutierrez aide says illegals are doing "essential jobs" and God help the economy if—spurred by our ingratitude—they go home. And what do we do with these largely uneducated, untrained workers if the economy heads south, as indicators suggest it might?

Instead of benefits, Americans are more apt to associate illegal immigration with words like crime, disease and loss of national identity. Contagious diseases like tuberculosis and leprosy are reappearing in this country, thanks to illegal immigration. Peter Brimlow, author of "Alien Nation," reports that several years ago, senior probation officers in Orange County, Calif., estimated that up to 80 percent of their cases involved illegals.

The Wrong Message to Send

Extending a blanket amnesty tells inhabitants of the impoverished Third World that if they can sneak past the Border Patrol, Uncle Softie will eventually welcome them with open arms.

It also says to those abroad patiently waiting for permission to immigrate (sometimes up to 18 years): "Suckers!"

The Immigration Reform and Control Act (IRCA) of 1986 granted amnesty to 2.8 million. According to the Immigration and Naturalization Service, there are more illegals in the country now.

Aliens granted amnesty can immediately sponsor their spouses and dependent children for residency. If they become citizens, they can sponsor parents and siblings.

It's difficult to get demographics on "undocumented workers." (If someone breaks into your house, is he an "uninvited guest"?) However, in 1992 the INS surveyed those given amnesty in 1986. Only 15 percent spoke English, though all had been here for at least a decade; 80 percent used public health services. On average, they had a seventh-grade education.

Political Calculations

Democrats support this dubious contribution to the general welfare, with a wink and a nod, because they directly benefit from the support of ethnic lobbies eager to increase their numbers.

IRCA Amnesty Admissions: 1989 to 1996

	Resident as of 1982	Agricultural Workers	Dependents	Total
1989	478,814			478,814
1990	823,704	56,668		880,372
1991	214,003	909,159		1,123,162
1992	46,962	116,380	52,272	215,614
1993	18,717	5,561	55,344	79,622
1994	4,436	1,586	34,074	40,096
1995	3,124	1,143	277	4,544
1996	3,286	1,349	184	4,819
Total	1,593,046	1,091,846	142,151	2,827,043

Federation for American Immigration Reform, 1997.

Republicans lack the courage to do anything positive about the problem, though most in Congress oppose mass amnesties. They are convinced that by keeping a low profile they can do better with the Hispanic vote.

In the 2000 campaign, President George W. Bush refused to support initiatives to end bilingual education or recognize English as our official language. He ended up with about 35 percent of the Latino vote and congratulated himself for improving the GOP position.

However, as the *National Review*'s John O'Sullivan notes, this still means that for every 100 illegal immigrants who come here (most from south of the border) and become citizens, the Republicans will have a net loss of 30 votes.

By not defending our sovereignty, Republicans miss an opportunity to appeal to the majority of Americans who understand that illegal immigration undermines national identity. (Bush took only 54 percent of the white vote in 2000.) It's also a way to court lower-income blacks, the chief victims of cheap illegal-immigrant labor.

On Feb. 16, 2000 Bush is scheduled to meet with Mexican President Vicente Fox, who will press him to be lenient with Mexicans who've infiltrated the United States. During the election, Dubya said, "I'm not prepared to embrace amnesty because I don't think the commitment's there yet to do anything on the border." This is Bush-speak for: We have to plug our porous border before we can consider compassion for lawbreakers.

Illegal immigration benefits the people of this country the way treason enhances national security.

"Granting birthright citizenship to the children of illegal aliens is misguided and just plain wrong."

America Should Not Grant Birthright Citizenship to Children of Illegal Immigrants

Tom Andres

The Fourteenth Amendment to the U.S. Constitution states that "all persons born or naturalized in the United States, and subject to the jurisdiction therof, are citizens of the United States." Passed in 1868 to secure U.S. citizenship for newly freed black slaves, it has been interpreted as sanctioning citizenship on children of illegal immigrants who are born in the United States. In the following viewpoint, Tom Andres questions this practice of bestowing birthright citizenship to children of illegal immigrants, arguing that such a policy encourages and rewards illegal immigration while sending a message that America is not serious about controlling it. Andres is a freelance writer who writes frequently on environmental topics.

As you read, consider the following questions:
1. What is the "anchor baby" effect of birthright citizenship, according to Andres?
2. How does the author respond to the contention that denying birthright citizenship is not compassionate?
3. What connection does Andres make between immigration and the environment?

From "End Birthright Citizenship," by Tom Andres, *The Social Contract*, Spring 1999. Copyright © 1999 by *The Social Contract*. Reprinted with permission.

In January, Rep. Brian Bilbray (R-CA) introduced the Citizenship Reform Act of 1999 (HR 73 IH) "to amend the Immigration and Nationality Act to deny citizenship at birth to children born in the United States of parents who are not citizens or permanent resident aliens." Representative Mark Foley (R-FL) is proposing a constitutional amendment (HJ RES 10) to accomplish the same thing. [Editor's note: neither measure passed.] These efforts should have our support because granting birthright citizenship to the children of illegal aliens is misguided and just plain wrong.

This automatic citizenship "right" is said to come from the Fourteenth Amendment's (1868) granting of citizenship to people "subject to the jurisdiction of the United States," which was intended strictly for former slaves. The "jurisdiction" language itself came from Senator Lyman Trumbull who authored some of the first legislation enfranchising freed slaves.

So it is hard to imagine how this amendment commands that citizenship be awarded to the children of illegal aliens. Even if we just look at the words, how can it be said that families who are defying the "jurisdiction" of the United States are also "subject to" it? If they are, well then, why are they here?

A Wrong Message

Birthright citizenship broadcasts a message that the United States is just not serious about enforcing its own immigration laws, a message further amplified by other government activities.

No doubt there exist some dedicated public servants struggling under conflicting and dubious political and judicial guidelines, but what a spectacle. Glance at any newspaper on any given day and you will see articles on "Stepped up border enforcement," or for this or that reasons, "Illegals freed," or "More aggressive employer raids," or "New toughness," or "Extended stays," until the whole enterprise starts looking as if it lacks only one big tent, two pachyderms and a brightly colored train before it can begin touring from town to town.

Birthright citizenship circumvents our overall immigration

policy, assuming we have one. It also assumes our policy-makers sometimes consider the impact of overall immigration numbers, including descendants, over time.

Each "anchor baby," as one expert points out, can then become "a demographic time bomb," since at age twenty-one he or she can petition for the admission of parents, siblings, spouses, spouses of siblings, children of siblings—forever chaining on and on down the line. This under-the-table immigration is occurring as others, who have had the tough luck of not having been born to illegals, wait for years to be admitted through standard channels.

Compassionate Policies?

Of course, when these subjects are brought up the Compassion Police immediately jump into their verbal squad cars and rush to the scene of argument. But a policy that refrains from bestowing citizenship on the children of illegals would no more be "blaming" or "punishing" innocent children than an airline would be blaming or punishing the children of hijackers by not awarding them Frequent Flier mileage for unscheduled flights to Havana.

The Children of Illegal Immigrants Should Not Be Granted Citizenship

Our current practice of granting automatic citizenship to the children of illegal immigrants . . . has no legal basis, and is the result of a misinterpretation of our laws. . . .

I do not blame young mothers for wanting to give their babies the option of a better life in America. However, the practice of granting automatic citizenship has established a powerful lure, while at the same time undermining our own immigration laws by rewarding illegal behavior.

Brian Bilbray, *San Diego Union-Tribune*, August 29, 1996.

What sort of compassionate nation says, "While you must not come here illegally, if you do somehow manage to sneak over the border, avoid arrest, survive stumbling across the desert a few days, snag some slave-wage job hidden in the shadows of our society, and then have a baby—Bingo!"?

Immigration scholars say that there are also significant

numbers of illegals who have no intention of becoming U.S. citizens. Apparently in those cases "compassion" takes the form of birthright law swopping into maternity wards and netting newborns into citizenship captivity. American citizenship was once highly prized. How low it has fallen in the eyes of our political leaders who now want to scatter it as widely as possible like cheap trinkets thrown to a crowd along a parade route.

This "child-citizen loophole"—estimated to add up to at least an extra million citizens—is yet another example of America trumpeting to the world that there really are no population limits to any nation's environmental carrying capacity. Hence the unofficial U.S. motto "Nature—Schmature—Let's Grow."

We are a mystery. It is doubtful that there has ever been a society so determined to rapidly overpopulate and deconstruct itself. But one significant step we can take in the opposite direction is to change this misguided policy of granting birthright citizenship to the children of parents who are, after all, citizens of other nations and who have decided to live in the United States illegally.

"No aspect of today's illegal immigration problem justifies an assault on the 14th Amendment."

America Should Grant Birthright Citizenship to Children of Illegal Immigrants

Jack Kemp

All children born within the United States (except children of foreign diplomats) are considered citizens, regardless of the status of their parents. Some people have objected to granting birthright citizenship to children of illegal immigrants, and have proposed federal legislation to change this practice. In the following viewpoint, Jack Kemp argues that such restrictions on citizenship are not the right way for the United States to respond to the problem of illegal immigration. Ending birthright citizenship would violate the U.S. Constitution and would do little to deter illegal immigration, he contends. Kemp, a former member of Congress and the Republican nominee for vice president in 1996, directs Empower America, a public policy and advocacy organization that he cofounded.

As you read, consider the following questions:

1. What benefits do immigrants bring to America, according to Kemp?
2. What alternatives to repealing birthright citizenship does the author recommend the nation should do regarding illegal immigration?
3. What practical problems would be created by repealing citizenship for children of illegal immigrants, according to Kemp?

G ood causes sometimes spawn bad ideas.
A case in point is a bill being discussed in Congress to fight illegal immigration by denying birthright citizenship to children born in America to illegal immigrant parents. This would violate the 14th Amendment to the Constitution, enacted 129 years ago [in 1868] to guarantee that all children born in America are granted citizenship with equal rights and protections under our laws.

America has every reason to stop illegal immigration. We should heed the words of Father Theodore Hesburgh [former president of the University of Notre Dame], who said that we must close the back door of illegal immigration in order to keep open the golden door of legal immigration.

In doing so, we will ensure that our laws are respected, while preserving the benefits immigrants bring to America: they fill key segments of the labor force, contribute to high-tech innovation, and serve as a "powerful source of vitality and stability in our distressed inner cities," according to Fannie Mae chairman James A. Johnson.

The bill, H.R. 7, is being considered in the House Immigration Subcommittee. [Editor's note: the bill was not passed.] It would end the constitutional guarantee that was put in place to prevent the revival of the Dred Scott decision of 1857, or any other means of excluding a class of Americans from full citizenship.

Enforce Existing Laws

There are many legitimate means to reduce illegal immigration, but violating a constitutional right is not among them. Rather than change the Constitution, Congress should concentrate on effective enforcement of immigration laws.

In 1996, Congress passed a new law that comprehensively addresses the issue of illegal immigration. Among its many provisions, the Illegal Immigration Reform and Immigrant Responsibility Act of 1996 increases border enforcement (it nearly doubles the size of the Border Patrol), increases penalties for alien smuggling, and makes it more difficult for visitors to overstay legal visas and become illegal immigrants. Congressional oversight of the Immigration and Naturalization Service is undoubtedly having a further positive impact on the total effort to stop illegal immigration, and to increase respect for immigration laws.

To my mind, it is doubtful that elimination of birthright citizenship would have a significant impact on illegal immigration, or that it would even touch the fundamental incentive that brings many illegal immigrants to America—the desire to work and improve their lives.

Practical Problems

Beyond its clear violation of the 14th Amendment, legislation to end birthright citizenship would create a new series of practical problems for citizens and government alike. Native-born Americans would have to prove their parents' citizenship in order to enjoy the rights and privileges of their own citizenship. This in turn would introduce new possibilities for racial and ethnic discrimination. A stateless class would be created—the first native-born non-citizens to grow up in America since the children of slaves before the Civil War.

Making Things Worse

Denying citizenship to the children of illegal immigrants would not ameliorate the problem it claims to address. In fact, it would more likely fulfill the worst fears of the anti-immigration forces—creating, out of people born within our borders, an unassimilable community of estranged aliens. It's hard to see how that could be an improvement on a policy that, by treating them as Americans, makes them Americans.

Stephen Chapman, *New Republic*, April 8, 1996.

Lastly, it is absolutely clear that legislative efforts to circumscribe the 14th Amendment would raise a series of doubts and concerns about the bedrock civil rights protections that have been enshrined in our Constitution since the Civil War.

No aspect of today's illegal immigration problem justifies an assault on the 14th Amendment. Everything in our character as Americans—regardless of our party affiliation, regardless of where we were born—should lead us to venerate and preserve the structure of civil rights protections that the struggle and sacrifice of Abraham Lincoln and countless Americans produced a century ago.

"If we fail to fix or replace the status quo, poor, immigrant workers will resort to more desperate means to sneak into our country."

America Should Admit Guest Farmworkers

Larry Craig

In the years during and after World War II, the United States permitted hundreds of thousands of agricultural workers from Mexico and other foreign nations to work temporarily in America. This "bracero" program was largely halted in the early 1960s. However, a very limited number of foreign farmworkers continued to be admitted under the federal "H-2A" program administered by the Labor Department. In the following viewpoint, Larry Craig, a U.S. senator from Idaho, argues that the United States should significantly increase the number of agricultural workers it allows to temporarily work in this country. Such a program would assure American farms of adequate labor and would alleviate the problem of exploitation of illegal farmworkers entering the United States. Craig, a Republican, was first elected to the Senate in 1990.

As you read, consider the following questions:
1. What difference does immigration status make to a farmworker, according to Craig?
2. What problems exist in current federal programs concerning guest farm workers, according to the author?
3. What crisis does Craig believe might be created if the farmworker status quo is continued?

Excerpted from Larry Craig's testimony before the U.S. Senate, Judiciary Committee, Subcommittee on Immigration, May 12, 1999.

W e are facing a problem today that will be a crisis tomorrow. This hearing is the first critical step the
Senate can take to do what our federal government does all
too rarely—fix a problem in a timely and common-sense
fashion before it inflicts great hurt on millions of Americans.

What We Need

Our agricultural growers want and need a stable, predictable, and *legal* work force, and they are happy to pay
good, fair, market-based compensation for it.

Unemployed workers and those hoping to move from
welfare to work want and need to be matched up with decent
jobs. American citizens should have first claim on American
jobs, but all workers would rather be working legally and
hope for the protection of basic labor standards.

These goals are not being met today. In fact, current federal law, and its bureaucratic implementation, are hurting
growers and workers. . . .

There is *no* debate about whether many—or most—farm
workers are immigrants. They are now, and they will be, for
the foreseeable future.

The question is whether they will be legally authorized to
work in America or not.

Immigrants *not* legally authorized to work in this country
know they must work in hiding. They can not assert their
rights, for fear that the U.S. government, the employer, or
the labor contractor can ignore them or retaliate.

In contrast, *legal* workers have legal protections. They ran
assert wage and other legal protections. They can bargain
openly and join unions. H-2A workers, in fact, are even
guaranteed housing and transportation.

That's a far cry from the plight of those working here *illegally*, who have been known to pay $1,000 and more to be
smuggled into the country.

In fact, the only group who has a stake in continuing the
status quo are "coyotes"—a minority of labor contractors,
who illegally smuggle workers into this country, often under
dangerous and inhumane conditions. Meaningful H-2A reform means we start putting criminals who trade in human
beings out of business.

The Status Quo Is Broken

The current H-2A Agricultural Guest Worker Program is profoundly broken.

The failure to fix or replace this program means that the federal government is completely ignoring the growing needs of a significantly changed agricultural labor market.

The status quo is a lose-lose-lose situation. It is bad for growers, bad for workers, and bad for American citizens and taxpayers who expect to have secure borders.

The status quo is breeding an underground economy that makes some of its victims hide from the rest of society and threatens to bankrupt the others.

H-2A Workers Entering the United States 1987–1996

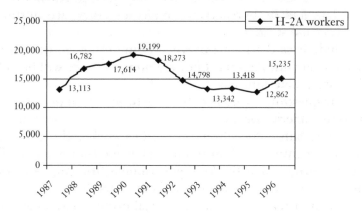

Statement of Demetrios G. Papademetriou before the U.S. Senate Subcommittee on Immigration, May 12, 1999.

Unlike many other sectors, farm and ranch work is often temporary, seasonal, and itinerant. This is not a matter of choice on anyone's part, but a matter of necessity.

Many of these jobs are filled by unauthorized immigrants. This, too, emphatically is not the desire of any employer. But our current laws and their enforcement have created worse than a Catch-22—for growers *and* for workers.

The employer is required to make sure prospective workers fill out an I-9 form and present what *appears* to be legitimate identification. However, beyond that, any inquiry into legal status is suspect under civil rights laws.

Therefore, many employers who meet the minimum and maximum legal standards of diligence when they hire a worker, really have no idea if the next raid by the Immigration and Naturalization Service, three counties away, will scare half or more of their work force into disappearing.

In fact, [a 1998] General Accounting Office [GAO] study estimated that as many as 600,000 farm workers—or 37 percent of 1.6 million—are not legally authorized to work in the United States.

In contrast, this year [1999] H-2A is expected to place only 34,000 legal guest workers—*two percent* of the total agricultural work force.

I want to put that number of known unauthorized workers—600,000 or 37 percent—into a practical perspective.

When Census-takers go door-to-door, they reassure interviewees that the personal information they collect will not be used for any other purpose by any other government agency—including deportation of illegal immigrants. Yet we've all heard innumerable stories and studies about how the Census under-counts unauthorized immigrants, because they hide from the Census-takers—the least-threatening of any information-collecting government employees.

Amazingly, the GAO figure of a work force that is 37 percent illegal concurs with Department of Labor estimates and is based on *self-disclosure* by unauthorized immigrants in government surveys.

This more-than-implies that the true number of farm workers who come here illegally is much higher than 37 percent—a number that is already astronomically high.

Costs on Employers

The H-2A status quo is complicated and fraught with legalistic risks. For farmers and ranchers who already deal with an over-complicated tax code, environmental laws, complex labor laws, and government bureaucracies in all areas from trade to commodity regulation to farm programs—the status quo requires them to hire yet another lawyer to digest the 325-page H-2A handbook plus cope with additional, unpublished, agency practices.

The H-2A status quo is slow, bureaucratic, and inflexible. It does nothing to recognize and adapt to the uncertainties farmers face. It requires growers to predict with perfect precision their labor needs months in advance, despite the challenges of changing weather, international and domestic markets, and individual worker needs.

And the H-2A status quo imposes unrealistic costs in the form of permanent capital investments in housing needed only temporarily, transportation costs that can be applied inequitably, and the far-above-market "Adverse Effect Wage Rate."

Finally, even the grower who lines up all those ducks well in advance, still can't count on his or her government to do its job as promised. The GAO study found that, in more than 40 percent of the cases in which employers filed H-2A applications at least 60 days before the date of need, the Department of Labor missed statutory deadlines in processing them.

Those are some of the reasons why the H-2A program today supplies about 34,000 workers, instead of 600,000. Today's program doesn't work.

Which brings us to the point of why H-2A reform is becoming a more critical necessity almost daily.

The Consequence of Inaction

If we do not reform H-2A, what will happen to the unauthorized 37 percent of the farm work force as we do a better and better job of controlling our borders?

Hundreds of thousands of workers will be pulled out of the agricultural labor pool.

There will be no effective way to replace them with legal workers.

Thousands of growers, already operating on the brink because of international economic problems, will have to give up the farm or go bankrupt.

If we fail to fix or replace the status quo, poor, immigrant workers will resort to more desperate means to sneak into our country. The farther underground they go means they will have less and less in the way of protection against exploitation from all sides. The "coyote" smuggling industry that already provides counterfeit documents and stealth transportation will escalate its illegal activities.

At the same time, as the number of legally available workers drops, crops will go unplanted or unharvested. We are already seeing spot shortages and localized crises because of these trends—from Washington State to Georgia, from California to New York.

Unless we fix the status quo, the domestic farm products that will no longer make it to the grocery store will be replaced by more and more imported food products.

I do not believe we, as a country, want to lose the ability to produce our own food supply. If we do, then the quality of the food we eat will be uncertain and the health and safety of our people will be put at risk.

The crisis may not appear this week or this month. But we should act before this situation becomes a crisis.

We will hear from those who think a little administrative tinkering will solve the problem. But Administrative band-aids will not help. In many cases, relying on administrative tinkering simply means asking the fox to reinvent the henhouse. . . .

The Solution Is in Sight

Reforming H-2A is the *most humane* alternative, for both workers and farmers. We want and need a stable, predictable, legal work force in American agriculture.

Willing American workers deserve a system that puts them first in line for available jobs with fair, market wages.

American consumers deserve a safe, stable, domestic supply of food.

American citizens and taxpayers deserve secure borders and a government that works.

All of these essential needs can be met if we fix or replace the H-2A guest worker program with one that provides an effective job-match system that provides *legal temporary*, immigrant workers when the need cannot be met by the domestic labor force.

We need a national AgJOBS registry . . . to match farmworkers with jobs. Domestic workers should be given preference. The job bank should verify the worker's legal status. If domestic workers are not available, using the job bank should qualify the farmer for expedited approval for hiring H-2A workers.

We need to make H-2A more flexible and economical, while maintaining basic worker protections. H-2A workers should be guaranteed at least the prevailing wage. Our already strapped farmers should have economic and flexible options in providing for the housing and transportation needs of H-2A workers.

We need to make sure any new program prevents overstays and makes our borders more secure. For those guest workers who follow the law, come here to work legally, and return home on schedule, if they want to immigrate to the United States someday, they should have some degree of preference.

I look forward to working with my colleagues, and all interested parties, to these ends.

"A new guestworker program . . . [will result in] large numbers of guestworkers who . . . will overstay their visas and exacerbate the problem of undocumented workers in this country."

America Should Not Admit Guest Farmworkers

Howard L. Berman

Many of the illegal residents in the United States work in agriculture. Some lawmakers have proposed creating or expanding programs in which workers from Mexico and other nations would be allowed to legally reside and work in the United States on a temporary basis. In the following viewpoint, Howard L. Berman, a California Democrat who has served as a member of the House of Representatives since 1982, opposes this idea. He argues that such a practice would drive down wages paid to farmworkers and would encourage "temporary" farmworkers to stay in the United States, resulting in a greater number of illegal immigrants. Berman concludes that employers should improve pay and working conditions to attract American workers.

As you read, consider the following questions:
1. Is there a shortage of farm labor, according to Berman?
2. Why does the author believe that a guestworker program will fail to solve the problem of illegal immigration?
3. What should employers do to attract workers, according to Berman?

Excerpted from Howard L. Berman's testimony before the U.S. Senate, Judiciary Committee, Subcommittee on Immigration, May 12, 1999.

For as long as I have served as an elected official, I have made it my business to try to improve the circumstances of American farmworkers, the most impoverished working people in the United States. I am convinced that proposals to make it easier for agricultural employers to bring in foreign guestworkers would accomplish exactly the opposite. . . . [Such proposals] would deprive American farmworkers of job opportunities they badly want, and exacerbate the problem of an oversupply of farm labor. The result can only be to further drive down the wages and working conditions of American farmworkers. . . .

There is no shortage of farm labor in this country. In the 104th Congress, in the wake of the resounding defeat of . . . [a] guestworker amendment in the House and questionable prospects for a similar amendment in the Senate, proponents of a new guestworker program relented and sought a General Accounting Office (GAO) study to determine whether there is a shortage of farm labor. The GAO released its report in December 1997, finding that "a widespread farm labor shortage does not appear to exist now and is unlikely in the near future." The ink was hardly dry when efforts commenced to disparage the report by the very interests that had sought it.

In my own state of California, the most significant agricultural producing region in the country, the unemployment figures in rural counties are staggering, double-digit virtually across the board. The same can be said in the agricultural areas of Texas and Florida as well. And while we can scarcely contemplate the difficulty of the migrant farmworker's existence, the fact is that migrant farmworkers *migrate* to wherever the jobs are. American farmworkers *want* those jobs that agricultural employers claim they cannot fill with American workers. Certainly we can do a better job of alerting farmworkers to available jobs, and employers to available workers, . . . but that is a far cry from saying we need to bring in more impoverished low skill workers from foreign countries.

Now I do at this juncture want to make one point very clear. I do not deny the fact that an unacceptable percentage of the agricultural labor workforce is undocumented, nor do

I condone it. The GAO estimated the percentage at 37 percent; just a few months ago [in 1999], a California study based on Department of Labor (DOL) data put the figure at 42 percent. But not for a second do I think that agricultural employers exactly have "clean hands" in lamenting this phenomenon. Dolores Huerta [co-founder of United Farm Workers] can give you countless examples of American farmworkers being turned away at job sites by agricultural employers who *prefer* foreign workers.

Better Solutions to Farm Worker Problems

Labor-intensive agriculture continues to expand under the assumption that government will make farm workers available when and where they are needed. Farm workers remain among the poorest U.S. workers, with most employed seasonally and earning $5,000 to $10,000 a year. Farm labor contractors are expanding their roles, serving as shock absorbers in a labor market rife with labor and immigration law violations.

But the solution to farm worker problems is not a guest worker program that leaves the farm labor system unchanged. Even most farmers concede that history would likely repeat itself if illegal immigration were to be controlled and there were no new guest worker program. Wages would rise, there would be a rapid adoption of labor-saving machinery and better ways to manage now more expensive workers, and some crops might migrate to lower-wage countries.

Government policy should push agriculture toward a sustainable 21st century future, not permit it to revert to a 20th century "Harvest of Shame" past.

Philip Martin, Center for Immigration Studies *Backgrounder*, April 2000.

Having lamented the increasing percentage of the workforce that is presently undocumented, is the solution to create an expanded guestworker program? Let me observe the obvious: the large number of undocumented farmworkers are not going anywhere, unless this committee wants to tell me that we are going to undertake in this country deportations on an unprecedented scale. Create a new guestworker program and, mark my words, we will then have the present undocumented workers *PLUS* large numbers of guestworkers who, if experience is any guide, will overstay their visas and exacerbate the problem of undocumented workers in this country.

Guestworkers Will Stay

Make no mistake, no matter how large a percentage of their wages you might propose to withhold as an incentive to return to their home country, guestworkers won't go back. They are invariably better off overstaying their guestworker visas and bleeding into our underground economy. The U.S. Commission on Immigration Reform (or Jordan Commission) in 1997 concluded that creating a new agricultural guestworker program, would be a "grievous mistake", and that it would only serve to increase illegal migration instead of replacing an illegal workforce. In light of all the efforts by the U.S. Congress and this subcommittee in particular to combat illegal immigration, I urge you not to approve legislation which will only exacerbate the problem. . . .

From the worker point of view, . . . not *adding* to the supply of workers, whether documented or undocumented, . . . would give farmworkers a chance of seeing an improvement in their deplorable wages and working conditions. I am convinced that what agricultural employers fear is not an impending shortage, but rather the possibility, should the border continue to tighten and employer sanctions be effectively enforced in agriculture, that they might be deprived of the gross *oversupply* of farm labor they presently enjoy. It is that oversupply which is the reason why the wages and working conditions of American farmworkers remain a national disgrace.

Underlying the argument for an agricultural guestworker program is the notion that farmworkers must be forever doomed to poverty and inequity. Why? Where is it written, in this free market economy, that agricultural employers need not improve wages and working conditions to attract and retain an adequate supply of work-authorized labor? Do not insulate these employers from the laws of supply and demand by enacting a new guestworker program. The American farmworkers who want these jobs have suffered enough. Let's not make it worse.

Periodical Bibliography

The following articles have been selected to supplement the diverse views presented in this chapter. Addresses are provided for periodicals not indexed in the *Readers' Guide to Periodical Literature*, the *Alternative Press Index*, the *Social Sciences Index*, or the *Index to Legal Periodicals and Books*.

George M. Anderson	"New Tides of Immigration," *America*, July 1, 2000.
Michael Barone	"Be Our Guest," *U.S. News & World Report*, May 7, 2001.
Roy Beck	"Rewarding Illegal Aliens," *Social Contract*, Spring 1999.
William Buchanan	"Amnesty—Shamnesty," *Social Contract*, Summer 1999.
Robert E. Burns	"Don't Slam Lid on the Melting Pot," *U.S. Catholic*, March 1997.
Stephen Chapman	"Birth Control," *New Republic*, April 8, 1996.
Linda Chavez	"What to Do About Immigration," *Commentary*, March 1995.
John Dillin	"Immigration Proposals Get Mixed Reviews," *Christian Science Monitor*, May 1, 2001.
Alan Fechter and Michael S. Teitelbaum	"A Fresh Approach to Immigration," *Issues in Science and Technology*, Spring 1997.
Samuel Francis	"New Policies Repeal Immigration Laws," *Conservative Chronicle*, March 31, 1999.
James O. Goldsborough	"Labor Joins the Charade," *Social Contract*, Spring 2000.
John B. Judis	"Huddled Elites: Bipartisan Law vs. Good Law," *New Republic*, December 23, 1996.
Robert A. McGraw	"Effective Enforcement of Immigration Law," *Social Contract*, Spring 1997.
John J. Miller	"Amnesty National—An Immigration Puzzle," *National Review*, March 20, 2000.
Marcus Stern	"A Semi-Tough Policy on Illegal Workers," *Washington Post*, July 13, 1998.
Mark K. Stricherz	"Bill of Wrath," *Nation*, May 11, 1998.
Daniel W. Sutherland	"Revinventing the Border," *Reason*, April 1999.

CHAPTER 4

Should U.S. Immigration and Refugee Policies Be Changed?

Chapter Preface

Immigration and refugee policy is the responsibility of the federal government. The most recent effort by Congress to enact comprehensive reforms in this area was in 1996, when the Illegal Immigration Reform and Immigrant Responsibility Act (IIRIRA) became law. The legislation contained several elements designed to prevent illegal immigration. It increased funding for more U.S. Border Patrol agents and authorized the building of new fences and detention facilities. It strengthened criminal penalties for immigrant smuggling and document fraud. It also contained several provisions designed to make it easier for the Immigration and Naturalization Service (INS) officials to exclude people claiming refugee status and to deport undocumented immigrants. For example, officers at U.S. ports of entry can deport anyone attempting to enter without proper documents who cannot demonstrate a "credible fear" of harm upon returning home. Those who can demonstrate such fear and therefore the need for political asylum can be jailed in INS facilities until a hearing is arranged.

Since its passage in 1996, IIRIRA and the way it has been implemented has come under criticism, both for being too harsh and for being too lenient. Immigrant rights advocates argue that the INS has become too zealous in its efforts to deter fraudulent asylum claims, and that people who come without proper papers are often the strongest candidates for political asylum. One result of IIRIRA is a dramatic increase in the number of detainees held by the INS. In 1994, 5,500 people were detained by the INS. By 2000 the INS prison population had grown to 20,000 in federal, private, and county detention facilities. Critics contend that many of those held are routinely denied legal protections and due process, such as bail hearings and judicial review, that are extended to American citizens. However, the INS has also been denounced for lax or incompetent enforcement of immigration and refugee laws, resulting in an overall increase in the number of illegal immigrants in the United States. The viewpoints in this chapter examine several avenues of reform in U.S. immigration and refugee policy.

"The entry-exit document reconciliation system is the only way to have an accurate . . . idea whether visitors from a given country are abusing our laws."

A Border Entry and Exit Control System Should Be Implemented

Federation for American Immigration Reform

Many foreigners who legally enter the United States on temporary work, student, or tourist visas end up illegally staying past the expiration of their visas. To help prevent this, in 1996 Congress passed the Illegal Immigration Reform and Immigrant Responsibility Act. Section 110 of the law contained a provision that required the Immigration and Naturalization Service (INS) to implement a computerized tracking system of all foreigners who enter and leave the country. In the following viewpoint, the Federation for American Immigration Reform (FAIR) defends Section 110 from its critics and argues that an automated entry and exit system at all ports of entry in the United States is fundamentally necessary to enforce immigration laws. FAIR is a public interest organization that works to stop illegal immigration and limit legal immigration.

As you read, consider the following questions:

1. How many legal entries by nonimmigrants occur in the United States, according to FAIR?
2. What accommodations need to be made for frequent cross-border travelers, in FAIR's view?

The United States has a major problem with visitors overstaying their visas, taking jobs and staying illegally as if they were immigrants. A chief reason for the problem is that we have no effective tracking system for visitors to our country. The most recent estimate of the Immigration and Naturalization Service (INS) is that about two-fifths of the five million illegal alien residents in the United States in 1996 had entered the country with nonimmigrant visas.

There are a tremendous number of legal entries every year of nonimmigrants—in fiscal year 1996 the number of nonimmigrant entries was 24.8 million—and our business and tourist visitors are an important part of our economy. Nevertheless, the large number is not sufficient reason for having no effective systematic tracking system. The number of credit card transactions in the United States each year dwarfs the number of visitors, yet no one would suggest that the number of credit charges was too large to keep track of.

At present there is only a partial record of nonimmigrant entries. Foreign visitors who arrive at airports and ports of entry are required to complete an entry record (form I-94) to present with their passport and visa. Although the visa requirement is waived for several countries that have been determined to have little or minor abuse, they still fill out the I-94 form on their arrival. In 1996, nearly half (45%) of all of the nonimmigrant entries were by persons admitted under the visa waiver program.

Section 110

As part of the immigration reform effort that resulted in the Illegal Immigration Reform and Immigrant Responsibility Act of 1996 (IIRAIRA), a provision was adopted that mandated that INS develop an automated capability to collect the data needed to identify visa overstayers. This provision addressed the gap in tracking information on visitors that was identified by the U.S. General Accounting Office (GAO) in a 1993 report on illegal aliens. Section 110 of IIRAIRA requires the INS to implement an automated entry and exit control system at the nation's ports of entry that will document the entry and departure of "every alien" arriving in and leaving the U.S. by September 30, 1998. This required data collection system is to include all noncitizens—nonimmigrants as well as immigrants residing in the United States who enter or depart at any port of entry.

Section 110 was added to the IIRAIRA legislation late in the legislative process, after hearings and committee debate. It apparently took by surprise some interests that are affected by the new requirement. One of the parties that seems to have been caught unawares was the Immigration and Naturalization Service (INS). The Canadian government and U.S. interests that cater to Canadian cross-border travelers were another, and the travel industry that carries international visitors was another.

Following issuance of the 1993 GAO report on the inadequacy of the INS nonimmigrant tracking capability, the INS launched a pilot program at the Philadelphia International Airport to test a new automated data collection system. Working with one airline, electronic data on arriving and departing passengers were given to the INS for entry into its Nonimmigrant Information System (NIIS). By the end of September 1997, 12,619 records had been recorded on incoming nonimmigrants and 6,835 records on departing passengers were received and matched with arrival records. The INS found that the system worked.

However, the INS testified to Congress in November 1997 that it wanted section 110 amended to remove the data collection requirement at sea ports and at land borders (Canada and Mexico). The INS said that it was not prepared to undertake that comprehensive a system because of a lack of resources. It asked for authorization for pilot studies of how the system could operate at entry and exit points other than airports. At the same time it said that it is prepared to go ahead with implementing the system at airports on the basis of its already completed study.

The Canadian Government also expressed reservations to the U.S. Government. It foresaw an unmanageable problem at the border if each of millions of Canadian border crossers were required to fill out a form I-94 and have it checked by the INS officials. They professed to see this causing hours of delay at the border. This argument resonated with northern-state merchants, who argued that delaying or discouraging

Canadian tourists would hurt the region's economy.

According to the INS the air industry also has expressed reservations about the new section 110 requirement. This presumably is due to the fact that to facilitate a speedy transfer of information on arriving passengers to the INS, the airlines have to assume an additional reporting requirement. So far, the INS has only asked the airline industry to supply it voluntarily the information in their computers on incoming passengers in the "Advance Passenger Information System (APIS)." Only some airlines have cooperated in the voluntary program, and the INS is apparently loathe to mandate compliance.

Why a Comprehensive Approach Is Essential

The Philadelphia airport pilot program demonstrates that the automated entry-exit system will work only if it is standardized for the country as a whole. If a passenger arrived in Philadelphia but left from a different airport, the entry record would end up unmatched by a departure record and would appear as a visa overstayer. Conversely, a departing passenger's entry record might not be found if the entry was at a different location. Similarly, if an international traveler arrives by air and departs by land, the capability must exist to record that departure and match it to the entry record if the control system is to work adequately.

I-94 forms are now required of arriving foreign travelers at all international airports and seaports and for those international travelers crossing land borders who intend to travel into the interior of the United States (beyond 25 miles of the border) or for protracted periods. However, the system has been badly flawed by the lack of systematic data collection, especially on departing passengers—which is the responsibility of the airline or shipping line. According to Michael Hrinyak, the INS Deputy Assistant Commissioner for Inspections, the current data collection effort at airports—the most effective link in the system at present—collects entry and exit data on only approximately 12 percent of all nonimmigrant travelers. The INS has no systematic system to collect I-94 forms from land border departing travelers.

It should be clear that accurate data on visa overstayers is

Visa Abuse Is a Serious Problem

Slightly more than half of the nation's illegal immigrants, including the vast majority in the New York area, casually enter the country as tourists, students or business people, and then simply overstay their visas.

And although the Immigration and Naturalization Service (INS) spends millions to patrol the southern border, the agency virtually ignores those illegal immigrants who, like Francis and Theresa, have walked in through the nation's front door.

"There is absolutely no deterrence," said David Simcox, a senior fellow of the Center for Immigration Studies in Washington, which favors restrictions on immigration. "There isn't much there to stop anyone."

In fact, the INS has no specific programs aimed at seeking out and deporting the 150,000 visitors a year who end up illegally settling here. In 1994, only about 600 people were deported for overstaying their visas, out of 39,000 deportations.

Ashley Dunn, *New York Times*, January 3, 1995.

---

essential to effective enforcement of the nation's immigration laws. This is especially important if the visa waiver program is to be continued. The entry-exit document reconciliation system is the only way to have an accurate and comprehensive idea whether visitors from a given country are abusing our laws and should, therefore, be more carefully scrutinized by U.S. consular officials overseas. The data collected in a comprehensive, automated system will reveal not only who is violating the immigration law, but also patterns among nationalities and types of visas, and ports of entry, magnitude of the problem and provide useful information to be able to launch efforts to find and deport the offenders and to design remedial procedures to diminish the problem.

Border Cards

FAIR wholeheartedly supports the objective of IIRAIRA section 110. At the same time it recognizes that there is a legitimate distinction between most international travelers to the United States and those travelers who live near the border and cross it on a daily or frequent basis for employment, shopping or visits. That distinction is the basis for the current system of border crossing cards for Mexican border residents. Card holders may cross into the United States without visas for periods of up to 48-hours as long as they are not traveling more than 25 miles in-land from the border. The Border Patrol operates controls on highways and common carrier terminals to enforce this provision. There seems to be little need to change this system by requiring these visitors to complete the I-94 form for each crossing. It is clear that it would be a major additional burden on the INS.

However, a Mexican or Canadian who wishes to travel into the United States for a longer period and/or beyond the border area must obtain a visa. That person, upon crossing the border must present the I-94 form and obtain an entry stamp in the passport. That same person or any other international traveler completing a trip to the United States is required to turn in the I-94 form upon leaving the country. The INS needs to develop a systematic process to remind travelers of that requirement and to collect the forms. This is true for the land borders with both Canada and Mexico. If local Mexican and Canadian crossers are exempt from the I-94 requirement, there should be no significant traffic tie-up as soon as the system becomes routine.

It is unacceptable that some common carriers are remiss in collecting I-94 forms from departing passengers. To improve cooperation INS must put teeth into current penalties for non-cooperation. Spot checks of passengers at departure gates—to identify lax airline compliance—would serve this purpose. It should be a requirement for doing business in the United States that common carriers provide electronically the input for the automated APIS entry-exit system. The data is already in the computers of the common carriers, and the only expense is likely to be a modest software design outlay to generate the reports in a form specified by the INS. The carrier then would have additional responsibility for reporting to the INS only if at check-in the data on the traveler proved to be incomplete or inaccurate.

The efforts currently underway in the Senate and the House to amend section 110 could have the effect of eviscerating the entire system. While local land border crossers could be exempt from a comprehensive automated entry-exit data system without compromising its effectiveness, the effort to entirely exempt land border crossers from the system leaves a loophole so wide that the system would be seriously weakened. Similarly, proposals to relegate to further study and experimentation any further implementation of the system for sea and land ports may have the effect of postponing indefinitely the installation of a comprehensive and effective record-keeping system to enforce the immigration law.

[Editor's note: In May 2000 Congress passed legislation that amended Section 110 to remove the requirement that data be collected on every entering and exiting alien; it authorized the creation of an integrated electronic data system utilizing information already being collected by government officials at U.S. ports of entry.]

"This . . . requirement . . . will not prevent illegal immigration, but will be expensive to implement and cause inordinate delays at border crossings."

A Border Entry and Exit Control System Should Not Be Implemented

Bronwyn Lance

In 1996, as part of broad immigration reform legislation, Congress mandated that the Immigration and Naturalization Service (INS) take steps to construct and implement a computerized system for recording every entry and exit by a foreign visitor. The requirement, known as Section 110, attracted much criticism. In the following viewpoint, Bronwyn Lance argues that requiring data collection from every alien visitor would do little to prevent illegal immigration, but instead would result in long delays at border crossings, decreased trade and tourism, and economic difficulties in communities bordering Mexico and Canada. Lance is a Senior Fellow with the Alexis de Tocqueville Institution, a social policy think tank.

As you read, consider the following questions:

1. How many people cross the U.S.-Mexican border, according to Lance?
2. Why would entry-exit controls be of little help in preventing illegal immigration or catching terrorists, in Lance's opinion?

From "The Traffic Jam and Job Destruction Act," by Bronwyn Lance, *AdTI Issue Brief # 171*, June 1999. Copyright © 1999 by the Alexis de Tocqueville Institution. Reprinted with permission.

New federal immigration requirements, set to take effect in less than two years, would create waiting lines up to seven miles long at America's borders, demand more processing time than there are minutes in the day, and dramatically reduce retail trade, particularly along the Canadian border. Since the economies of the United States, Canada and Mexico are inextricably connected, the enormous shipping and traffic delays caused by this system could result in the loss of tens of thousands of jobs in Michigan, Texas, California, and other states along our northern and southern borders. Also, many manufacturing jobs—jobs that rely on timely shipments—in other parts of America and jobs in the tourism industry would be lost.

Section 110 of the 1996 immigration law, the Illegal Immigration Reform and Immigrant Responsibility Act (IIRAIRA), compels the Immigration and Naturalization Service (INS) to introduce an entry and exit control system "for every alien departing the United States, and match the records of departure with the record of the alien's arrival in the United States." The INS is required to implement such a system at land borders and sea ports, which is a departure from current law.

This new requirement, made with little forethought, will not prevent illegal immigration, but will be expensive to implement and cause inordinate delays at border crossings for both persons and transport. Additionally, the new law will not affect drug enforcement or terrorism prevention, and shows a willful disregard for America's diplomatic agreements with our neighbors.

A broad coalition of organizations are seeking the repeal of Section 110, including the U.S. Chamber of Commerce, the Travel Industry of America, the Border Trade Alliance, and over 200 companies and associations. . . .

Section 110

The 1996 omnibus immigration bill that included Section 110 was a vast piece of legislation affecting many aspects of our complex immigration law, from asylum to alien smuggling to welfare reform. Because of this, it is not surprising that parts of this legislation had some unintended consequences, several provisions of which have already been modified by the 105th Congress.

Section 110, while a small part of that legislation, will have dire consequences for trade between the U.S., Canada and Mexico, as well as for the states on our northern and southern borders. This provision provides that, by September 30, 1998, the Attorney General must develop an automated entry and exit control system that will enable the INS to track the arrival and departure of "every alien" entering and leaving the U.S. In 1998, a provision repealing the requirement for such a system passed the Senate in two different forms, but, due to opposition from the House immigration chairman, a 30-month delay, rather than an outright repeal, is what became law. This amended version of the original law only served to move the implementation date to March 2001.

On the surface, such a requirement might not appear onerous. However, because Section 110 specifically states that such a system would apply to "every alien," the Attorney General must develop these entry and exit controls to apply not only at airports, but at all ports of entry into the United States, including land borders and seaports. Currently, a paper-based entry and exit control system is in place and used mainly at airports.

This problematic section of the 1996 law, as originally drafted, called for a pilot program at airports to track visitors and to test the viability of expanding such a system in the future. The mandated checks on "every alien" entering and leaving the U.S. at all ports of entry was not debated in the House or the Senate. Instead, they were added just before finalization of the bill by conferees with little thought as to the impact such a system would have on trade, border communities and tourism. As Senate Judiciary Committee Chairman Orrin Hatch (R-UT) subsequently stated, "I think that we all have come to realize that Section 110 of the 1996 Act [was] inserted into the conference with little or no record, [and] no consideration or debate. It was well intended, there is no question, but I think poorly constructed."

Border Crossing Delays

Only after the enactment of IIRAIRA did the full impact of Section 110 become apparent. The INS, which has enough difficulty implementing the system currently in place, cannot implement an entry-exit system of this scope without causing extreme delays. The problem is not lack of INS resources and manpower, but rather that each person crossing the border will have to be stopped and interviewed.

According to some experts, even with the best and most efficient system possible in place at land border crossings, delays would be such that the borders between the U.S., Mexico and Canada would in effect, be shut down. In Senate testimony, Dan Stamper, president of the Detroit International Bridge Company, attested that the Ambassador Bridge handles approximately 30,000 vehicle crossings per day between the U.S. and Canada. Mr. Stamper testified that "assum(ing) the most efficient and remarkable entry and exit procedures in the world (that) will take only 30 seconds" per vehicle, and making another optimistic assumption that only half of those vehicles would have to go through the procedures, that would amount to "3,750 minutes of additional processing time each day." As there are only 1,440 minutes in a day, the implementation of Section 110 would mean that an already crowded border would effectively be closed.

The U.S.-Mexican border handles an even greater volume of traffic. Approximately 254 million people, 75 million cars and 3.5 million trucks cross the southern border at land points of entry each year.

In further congressional testimony, an analysis of the projected impact a mere pilot program of entry-exit controls would have on the Thousand Island Bridge between New York and Ontario showed that delays could be as much as two and a half days. The line of waiting vehicles would be more than 7 miles long.

Adverse Effects on Trade and Diplomacy

States with border communities that rely on cross-border trade and tourism would also be adversely affected. Among the states, Michigan is Canada's largest trading partner and is the fourth leading destination of Canadian tourists, behind New York, Washington, and Florida. Approximately 2.75 million Canadians visit New York State for at least one night, spending over $400 million. If border inconveniences arise, those Canadians may well choose to spend their dollars elsewhere. Trade will be adversely affected at the already congested U.S.-Mexico border. Our trade with Mexico exceeded $130 billion in 1996, the majority of which crossed the land border.

A Poorly Constructed Mandate

However well intentioned this provision [Section 110] seemed at the time, it is quite clear that it was poorly constructed. The theory behind the mandated system is far ahead of current technology. The Immigration and Naturalization Service admits that it cannot implement such a system. And, the creation of intolerable border delays would slow both travel and trade. NTA [National Tour Association] tour operators conducting tours requiring a border crossing already are confronted with significant delays. New and longer delays at land ports will be a further hindrance to commerce and impose high costs on companies that depend on trade and tourism with Canada and Mexico.

National Tour Association, "Issue Paper on Section 110," 2000.

The State Department has expressed concern that the implementation of Section 110 at land borders will harm our diplomatic relations with Canada and Mexico. It has been the long standing policy of the United States not to require any special documentation for Canadians entering the country. Letters from the ambassadors of both nations indicated their concern at the negative impact such entry-exit controls would have on the goodwill that exists among the U.S., Mexico and Canada, and on the large volume of cross-border trade.

Illegal Immigration and Terrorism

Section 110 would have a minimal impact on controlling illegal immigration and visa overstayers. While the collection of data on when aliens enter and exit the country can be useful when analyzing, for example, from which countries visa overstayers are likely to come, the benefits of such data in tracking down particular individuals who have overstayed their allotted time in the U.S. is questionable and uncertain. Since 1992, the INS has been unable to produce useable data from the paper-based entry-exit control system currently in place at airports. With such a track record, it is doubtful that the INS would keep consistent departure records, that the entry of names was accurate, or that the system was matching names correctly. Such a system is likely to be fraught with errors and be unreliable.

The argument has been made by proponents of Section 110 that it will aid in the fight against terrorism. However, given the likelihood of INS data entry errors, such an entry-exit control system would be sieve-like in its effectiveness. Also, the instance of fraud with this system would be high, as an individual intending to stay in the United States could easily have someone else fill out the overstayer's information on his exit card. The same scenario is possible with electronic identification. Additionally, even if there was a list of names and passport numbers of individual visa overstayers, there would be no useful information as to where individuals could be located. Terrorists seeking to avoid entry into the proposed entry-exit system would merely have to leave before their lawful period of entry, typically six months, has expired. Such a system will, at best, provide information only on those who have overstayed their visas, with no assistance in identifying terrorists, drug traffickers or other aliens who might be engaged in unlawful activities. If anything, the new required system is likely to undermine efforts to halt drug smuggling and terrorism, because if implemented, it would divert potentially billions of dollars for law enforcement efforts aimed at directly dealing with those concerns. . . .

No Evidence of Help

There is a significant problem with visa overstayers in the United States. However, the entry-exit system mandated by Section 110 will not solve this problem. Instead, it will significantly impede cross-border trade and tourism; cause grave economic harm to communities on both sides of the borders; engender ill-will with our neighbors; and has the potential for significant job destruction in trade-related and tourist-related industries. There is no evidence that this system will have any effectiveness on stopping terrorism, drug trafficking, or halting the increasing problem of illegal immigration and visa overstayers.

[Editor's note: In May 2000 Congress passed legislation that amended Section 110 to remove the requirement that data be collected on every entering and exiting alien; it authorized the creation of an integrated electronic data system utilizing information already being collected by government officials at U.S. ports of entry.]

"A labor migration pact would effectively recognize that . . . undocumented immigration cannot completely be halted."

The United States Should Consider Opening Its Borders to Mexican Workers

Kevin R. Johnson

Mexico is the leading country of origin for both legal and illegal immigrants to the United States, notes Kevin R. Johnson in the following viewpoint. He argues that the two countries should negotiate agreements dealing with labor migration, and recognize that efforts to stop illegal immigration are futile because of the allure of jobs and family ties. Johnson, a law professor, directs the Chicana/o Studies Program at the University of California, Davis.

As you read, consider the following questions:
1. What four principles should form the basis of U.S. immigration law, according to Johnson?
2. What does the author believe about the viability of an open borders policy?
3. How is the situation between the United States and Mexico comparable to the European Union, according to Johnson?

Excerpted from "Legal Immigration in the 21st Century," by Kevin R. Johnson, *Blueprints for an Ideal Legal Immigration Policy*, 2001. Copyright © 2001 by the Center for Immigration Studies. Reprinted with permission.

The following proposals for reform of U.S. immigration law operate on the following basic principles.

Basic Principles

First. Consistent with modern civil rights sensibilities in the United States, our immigration laws should not discriminate on the basis of race or national origin. Nor should the laws seek to shield the nation from the racial, ethnic, religious, and cultural diversity found throughout the world. Such discrimination has no place in the U.S. immigration laws or in their enforcement.

Second. In fashioning effective legal immigration proposals, immigration law and policy must take into account undocumented immigration. When the demand for migration far outstrips the numbers of immigrants who may be lawfully admitted, undocumented immigration, either through visa overstays and violations or through entries without inspection, will flourish. For example, if per country limits delay the immigration of nationals of certain countries with family in the United States for lengthy periods, those immigrants-to-be will have strong incentives to circumvent the immigration laws. Similarly, if the refugee admissions program remains inaccessible to citizens of nations embroiled in political violence, such as El Salvador and Guatemala in the 1980s and Haiti in the 1990s, persons from those countries will flee, often to the United States, regardless of the law. A coherent immigration policy must take into account modern political, economic, and social realities, including the pressures of undocumented immigration.

Third. Mexico is the leading country of origin of legal and undocumented immigrants to the United States. Regularizing the flow of immigrants—particularly undocumented immigrants—from Mexico obviously is critical to making a legal immigration system work effectively and efficiently. Importantly, regional migration pressures in an increasingly globalizing world economy appear unlikely to subside in the foreseeable future. The ideal legal immigration system must account for these pressures.

Fourth. We must strive to integrate all immigrants into the political, economic, and social fabric of American life.

To accomplish that goal, however, the U.S. government should not demand that immigrants "assimilate" or "Americanize"—ill-defined terms that carry emotional baggage among certain national origin minorities because of the unfortunate history of mandatory assimilation programs. We instead should strive to ensure respect for the cultures of immigrants and naturalized citizens and to guarantee equal citizenship for all in the United States.

Proposals

Under current political conditions in the United States, an open borders policy does not appear politically viable. Assuming that the political process demands limits on immigration, we must ensure that such limits do not invidiously discriminate and that the U.S. government does not selectively enforce the laws against citizens of certain nations.

Current Law. Current law recognizes four basic categories of immigration: family, employment, diversity, and refugee. In addition, several forms of relief from removal allow for-

© Joe Sharpnack. Reprinted with permission.

eign citizens in the country to secure lawful immigrant status. I offer two possible alternatives, which if properly crafted could work in tandem, to the current system: (1) a labor migration agreement between the United States and Mexico; and (2) a point system for allocating immigrant visas.

Alternative 1: Labor Migration Agreement Between the U.S. and Mexico. Reform of the legal immigration system will prove effective only if we are able to regularize labor migration from Mexico to the United States. As a nation, we must seriously consider a labor migration agreement between the United States and Mexico, combined with efforts to develop the Mexican economy in order to reduce economic incentives for Mexican citizens to leave their homeland.

As Europe has come to realize with the evolution of the European Union, trade and migration between neighboring nations are inextricably linked. A labor migration arrangement has worked relatively well in the European Union, which for the most part permits labor migration between member nations.

A Missed Opportunity

Although the United States, Canada, and Mexico entered into the North American Free Trade Agreement in 1994, the countries missed a historic opportunity to squarely address labor migration. Formidable challenges to a labor migration agreement between the United States and Mexico include the fact that the economic disparities and cultural differences between the peoples of those nations appear more dramatic than those between the populations of the member nations of the European Union. We must overcome the fears of these differences and the belief that a "flood" of immigrants from Mexico will come if given the opportunity.

A labor migration agreement between the United States and Mexico should not include a numerical cap, although it might require proof of employment or self-sufficiency for a migrant to enter the United States. A labor migration pact would effectively recognize that, absent draconian enforcement measures inconsistent with a modern constitutional democracy, undocumented immigration cannot completely be halted. The allure of jobs, combined with the pull of family and social networks established by generations of migration from Mexico to the United States, remains too strong.

Alternative 2: A Point System. For migration not covered by a regional agreement, a simple point system, allocating points based on family ties, educational attainment, employment skills, and related factors, with foreign citizens with certain point totals eligible for an immigrant visa, would represent an improvement over the current system. Canada's point system offers a ready model. However, while Canada's system focuses primarily on employment skills, an American version should allocate points more heavily on family reunification, the central organizing principle of the current immigration laws.

"The United States cannot act as a sponge for Mexico's poor."

Immigration from Mexico Should Be Limited

Robert J. Samuelson

Many of America's immigrants, both legal and illegal, come from the neighboring country of Mexico. Vicente Fox, elected president of Mexico in 2000, created a stir when he suggested that the two countries agree to more liberal border and migration policies and to legalize the movement of Mexican workers into the United States. In the following viewpoint, Robert J. Samuelson argues that while it might be in Mexico's interests to increase Mexican immigration to the United States, such immigration is not in America's interests. The United States does not need the poor and unskilled immigrants that Mexico would provide, Samuelson contends. Furthermore, allowing more migration from Mexico would harm Mexican immigrants already in the United States and would threaten to divide American society along ethnic lines. Samuelson is a columnist and contributing editor to *Newsweek* magazine.

As you read, consider the following questions:

1. What kind of immigrants does the United States need, in Samuelson's view?
2. How have immigrants from Mexico differed from past American immigrants, according to the author?
3. What argument does Samuelson make concerning the North American Free Trade Agreement (NAFTA)?

Americans ought to hope for the success of Vicente Fox Quesada, the new president-elect of Mexico. He broke the 71-year rule of the Institutional Revolutionary Party (PRI), creating a broader and more genuine democracy. He promises to attack corruption, curb the drug trade, encourage private investment and increase economic growth. Fox deserves our support and sympathy. But we should not let good will slip into sentimentality. American and Mexican interests sometimes collide—on immigration, for instance, where Fox seems to have large ambitions.

Opposing Interests

Our interest lies in less immigration from Mexico, while Mexico's interest lies in more. The United States has long been an economic safety valve for Mexico: a source of jobs for its poor. By World Bank estimates, perhaps 40 percent of Mexico's 100 million people have incomes of less than $2 a day. The same desperate forces that drive people north mean that, once they get here, they face long odds in joining the American economic and social mainstream.

The United States may (or may not) need more immigrants—this is a subject of much disagreement. But we surely don't need more poor and unskilled immigrants, and Mexicans fall largely in this category. The stakes here transcend economics. Americans are justly proud of being a nation of immigrants. Peoples of many lands and customs have become American—which is different from what they were—even as they refashioned what it means to be American. By contrast, many Mexican immigrants have little desire to "join the American mainstream" precisely because their overriding motive for coming was economic and their homeland is so close. Their primary affection remains with Mexico.

This is understandable, even commendable. (In 1997 only 15 percent of the estimated 7 million Mexican immigrants had become U.S. citizens. One reason, of course, is that perhaps 3 million are thought to be illegal.) But it is equally understandable that most Americans wish to preserve the nation's immigrant heritage—and not become simply a collection of peoples, from various places, who happen to work here and whose main allegiances lie elsewhere.

Fox's basic diagnosis of the immigration problem is sound. He believes that only greater prosperity in Mexico—more jobs, higher incomes—can reduce the flows. If people live better, they will stay home. Beginning in 1996, Mexico's economy has grown about 5 percent annually. Fox aims to raise that to 7 percent by 2006. He talks, somewhat inconsistently, of ultimately having open borders between the United States and Mexico, much as exist between members of the European Union. At one point, he says this could occur in a decade. At another point, he concedes it would require a convergence of incomes (perhaps 7 to 1 in America's favor) to prevent a mass exodus of Mexicans. Optimistically, that would take decades.

A Suggested Bargain

Meanwhile, he apparently hopes to raise legal immigration. This is the gist of various press leaks. He seems to suggest a bargain: the United States would allow more legal immigration; in return, Mexico would crack down—as it hasn't in the past—on illegal immigration. Already, Mexico is the largest source of legal immigrants, representing about 20 percent in 1998. The *Wall Street Journal* quotes one Fox adviser as saying that legal visas should increase by about 180,000, which would more than double their 1998 level.

For the United States, this would be a bad bargain. No one knows the number of Mexicans who come and stay illegally each year. The Immigration and Naturalization Service's last estimate (which dates from 1996) is 150,000. If this is correct, the proposed increase in legal visas would exceed the present number of illegal immigrants. Overall immigration would rise even if—miraculously and implausibly—illegal immigration stopped altogether.

The United States cannot act as a sponge for Mexico's poor. In the present boom, immigration is an issue easily forgotten. Anyone can get a job, we say. Immigrants (it's argued) have helped prevent a wage-price spiral. Up to a point, they may have. But the boom won't last forever, and the least-skilled immigrants always struggle.

The most obvious consequence of allowing more Mexican immigrants into the country would be to hurt those already here. The two groups clearly compete. An increase of

10 percent in new immigrants can reduce the wages of earlier immigrants by 9 or 10 percent, says a report from the Urban Institute in Washington. Fewer than half of Mexican-Americans over 25—including those born in the United States—were high-school graduates in 1996, according to a study from the National Council of La Raza, an advocacy group for Latinos. The same report warns that workers with poor English can do only "basic tasks at entry-level positions offering low wages." All this is common sense.

Fox's Vision

[Mexican president Vicente Fox] proposes that we create a European Union-style partnership in North America in which the U.S. and Canada would help create jobs and raise income levels in Mexico. Its implementation might be great for Mexico and eventually for all the nations of South America and the Caribbean, but would probably cause grave civil and economic problems for the United States. Reason: a mainstay of the EU concept is to do away with internal borders and custom posts. That means we would have to surrender control over our borders to allow into our country millions of Mexicans, followed in the ensuing years by millions of other Hispanics, most of whom would be poor and illiterate. This massive migration would take place regardless of the effect it would have upon our health, education and welfare systems our native labor force and, too, to our increasingly fragile environment.

Denos P. Marvin, *Social Contract*, Fall 2000.

The power of America's economy, culture and society to assimilate immigrants is enormous. History is clear: the children of immigrants increasingly become American. But that power is not unlimited. The job market, schools and social services can be overwhelmed by large numbers, especially—as is the case with Mexicans—when most immigrants come to only two states, California and Texas. The dangers are balkanizaton—a society increasingly fractured along class and ethnic lines—and a backlash against immigration. A possible perverse side effect is a rise in prejudice against Hispanic-Americans, who are confused for immigrants, even though they've often lived here for generations. This has long concerned civil-rights groups, like La Raza.

There is a difference between having open borders for goods and for people. The theory of NAFTA (the North American Free Trade Agreement) was that both the United States and Mexico could prosper from more trade and international investment. The theory remains powerful, even if it's no instant panacea for all of Mexico's problems. Vicente Fox and the next U.S. president have plenty of areas where they can cooperate to mutual advantage. But higher Mexican immigration isn't one of them.

"Whatever the theoretical benefits of temporary protection, it is clear that in the real world there is nothing as permanent as a temporary refugee."

U.S. Refugee Policies Encourage Illegal Immigration

Mark Krikorian

The United States has several programs under which it admits refugees from other nations or grants political asylum to foreigners residing in the United States. Under one such program created as part of the Immigration Act of 1990, foreigners visiting the United States can apply for "temporary protected status" (TPS) if armed conflict, natural disasters, or other extraordinary conditions make a return to their home country impossible or dangerous. In the following viewpoint, Mark Krikorian argues that the TPS program is a misnomer because "temporary" refugees invariably become permanent U.S. residents. The existence of such a program, he contends, has become a magnet for illegal immigration as people apply for TPS status but then lobby to remain in the United States. Krikorian is executive director of the Center for Immigration Studies, a research organization based in Washington, D.C.

As you read, consider the following questions:
1. How did U.S. policy toward Kosovar Albanian refugees evolve, according to Krikorian?
2. What was the chief reason why Congress created TPS in 1990, in the author's view?
3. What example does Krikorian provide of how temporary protection serves as a magnet for illegal immigration?

Temporary protection for foreigners in distress has figured prominently in discussions of immigration policy for some time. Hondurans, Kosovar Albanians, and Colombians are only the most recent groups considered for some kind of limited safe haven. Temporary protection amounts to a limited grant of refugee status, offering foreigners who would not otherwise be allowed to remain in the United States limited sanctuary until an emergency (civil war, widespread violence, or natural disaster) in their home country passes. For the most part, temporary protection has been offered to aliens already in the United States, usually illegally, who do not qualify for asylum but whom we are unwilling to deport.

As attractive as temporary protection seems on the surface, there is an enormous, and unbridgeable, gap between the theory and the reality. Forty years of experience have shown that "temporary" protection almost always results in permanent settlement. Whatever the theoretical benefits of temporary protection, it is clear that in the real world there is nothing as permanent as a temporary refugee.

Kosovar Albanians

The changing policy toward settlement of the Kosovar Albanians neatly illustrates this gap between theory and reality. Though most of the Kosovo Albanians were brought legally from overseas, rather than already here illegally, the principle of temporary protection was still the initial model applied to their situation.

During the Sunday morning talk shows on April 4, 1999, it was revealed that the United States would provide temporary sanctuary to 20,000 Kosovar Albanians at our naval base at Guantanamo Bay in Cuba, as part of a broader effort by Western countries to move Kosovar Albanians fleeing Serbian attacks out of an untenable situation in Macedonia. Because Guantanamo is on foreign soil, the Kosovar Albanians would not be able to claim asylum or enter the United States. . . .

Within days, hints began to emerge from the White House that the Kosovars might not be sent to Guantanamo after all, prompted by complaints from refugee-service groups that the refugees would be isolated on the remote naval base. Then, in an April 21 speech at Ellis Island, Vice President [Al] Gore announced that the Kosovar Albanians would be resettled as refugees in the U.S.: "We will accept, on the American mainland, up to 20,000 of the hurting and homeless Kosovar refugees—those with close family ties in America and those who are vulnerable. . . . We will bring them here until they are able to return home safely." But Gore continued to insist that the refugees' stay would be temporary: "We anticipate their return to Kosovo. . . . the ones coming to the United States, will also be prepared to return on short notice."

By the next day, however, administration officials conceded the obvious—that many of the Kosovar Albanians would obtain permanent residence in the United States, a benefit available after one year to anyone admitted as a refugee. In the words of a senior administration official, "We are going to try to create conditions in Kosovo for these people to return, but the choice will ultimately be theirs." Rep. Eliot L. Engel (D-N.Y.), chairman of the House Albanian Issues Caucus, put it more plainly: "And let's face it, after a year or two, they'd have had a taste of political freedom. They won't want to go back. . . . The reality is that the vast majority are probably here to stay."

First planeload of 453 Kosovar Albanians arrived at Fort Dix, N.J., on May 5; the first baby was born on American soil hours later. The war ended before the 20,000 quota was filled, and a total of about 10,000 people were eventually resettled in the United States. By the end of [the] summer [of 1999], only about 10 percent will have returned to Kosovo.

This shift from temporary to permanent relocation for the Kosovar Albanians was remarkable mainly for the speed with which it happened. Otherwise, it is simply another instance of temporary status leading to permanent settlement. And how could it be otherwise? After a long period of residence, any alien, however "temporary" his nominal status, will put down permanent roots in the community that make it increasingly difficult to deport him—he may marry, have children, start a business, buy a home, and at some point it becomes politically, and perhaps even morally, untenable to ask him to leave.

Origins of Temporary Protection

Legislation to create a formal process for temporary protection was debated and voted on in Congress at various points in the late 1980s, but was not enacted into law until "Temporary Protected Status" (TPS) was created by the Immigration Act of 1990. Prior to the creation of this status, there was no statutory basis for permitting illegal aliens, or nonimmigrants whose visas were expiring, to remain in the United States without requesting asylum. But as early as 1960, the executive branch created "Extended Voluntary Departure" (EVD) as a temporary grant of blanket relief from deportation for nationals of certain countries who feared returning to their homelands. EVD was justified as an exercise of prosecutorial discretion by the Attorney General in deciding not to force the departure of certain aliens. (See Table 1 below for grants of EVD.)

Table 1. Nationals from the Following Countries Received EVD During the Years Listed:	
Cuba	1960–1966
Dominican Republic	1966–1978
Czechoslovakia	1968–1977
Chile	1971–1977
Cambodia	1975–1977
Vietnam	1975–1977
Laos	1975–1977
Lebanon	1976
Ethiopia	1977–1982
Hungary	1977–1981
Romania	1977–1981
Uganda	1978–1986
Iran	1979
Nicaragua	1979–1980
Afghanistan	1980–1985
Poland	1982–1989

Federal Register, INS

The transition to permanent residence of "temporary" refugees was present from the start. In the 1960s, the thousands of Cubans fleeing Castro's regime were allowed to stay under EVD until Congress passed the Cuban Adjustment Act in 1966, which granted them, and thousands to follow, the right to remain permanently. In the 1970s, thousands fled the communist takeover of Indochina, and they too were granted EVD until Congress in 1977 made their status permanent. And in 1987, more than 5,000 people from Afghanistan, Ethiopia, Poland, and Uganda who had EVD were granted amnesty by Congress in legislation championed by Sen. Jesse Helms (R-N.C.).

In April 1990, [former] President [George] Bush issued Executive Order 12711 giving an estimated 80,000 nationals of the People's Republic of China temporary protection from deportation, as a result of the 1989 government crackdown on democracy activists there. Afraid that a grant of EVD to those fleeing a left-wing regime could be used as a precedent to demand EVD for those fleeing the friendly right-wing regime in El Salvador, the administration made up a new status, "Deferred Enforced Departure," which was an administrative stay of deportation ordered by the president. DED was, for all intents and purposes, identical to EVD. The final result was the same as well—in 1992, Congress passed the Chinese Student Protection Act, which made this temporary status permanent by allowing Chinese who entered before the issuance of the executive order to apply for a green card. Though students were supposed to be the beneficiaries of this legislation, a large number—perhaps the majority—of those receiving green cards were actually illegal aliens from the province of Fujian, smuggled into the United States by "snakehead" gangs.

TPS Defined in Statute

Finally, in 1990, Congress passed the Immigration Act which, among other things, empowers the Attorney General to grant Temporary Protected Status to people whose countries are suffering war or natural disaster. The relevant section of the Immigration and Nationality Act reads:

> *The Attorney General, after consultation with appropriate agencies of the Government, may designate any foreign state (or any part of such foreign state) under this subsection only if—*
>
> *(A) the Attorney General finds that there is an ongoing*

armed conflict within the state and, due to such conflict, re-
quiring the return of aliens who are nationals of that state to
that state (or to the part of the state) would pose a serious
threat to their personal safety;

(B) the Attorney General finds that—

> *(i) there has been an earthquake, flood, drought, epidemic,*
> *or other environmental disaster in the state resulting in a*
> *substantial, but temporary, disruption of living conditions in*
> *the area affected,*

> *(ii) the foreign state is unable, temporarily, to handle ade-*
> *quately the return to the state of aliens who are nationals of*
> *the state, and*

> *(iii) the foreign state officially has requested designation un-*
> *der this subparagraph; or*

(C) the Attorney General finds that there exist extraordinary
and temporary conditions in the foreign state that prevent aliens
who are nationals of the state from returning to the state in
safety, unless the Attorney General finds that permitting the
aliens to remain temporarily in the United States is contrary to
the national interest of the United States.

(Interestingly, this last provision puts the Attorney General in the perverse position of determining that it is in the national interest to allow illegal aliens to reside in the United States.)

The chief impetus behind the creation of TPS was the government's unwillingness to deport thousands of illegal aliens from El Salvador, which was engulfed in civil war during much of the 1980s. In fact, section 303 of the Act specifically designated Salvadorans for TPS. Almost 200,000 illegals were thus able to avoid deportation for a period of 18 months. However, when the Salvadorans' TPS expired in 1992, the administration still chose not to deport them and simply reverted to the old practice of granting ad hoc status, this time re-using the label Deferred Enforced Departure.

Though DED for Salvadorans ended in 1996, there is little prospect of their deportation. The 1990 settlement of a class-action lawsuit allows Salvadorans protected under TPS and DED to re-apply for asylum on the grounds that their previous asylum applications had allegedly not been given proper consideration for political reasons. In addition, the

Nicaraguan Adjustment and Central American Relief Act of 1997 (NACARA) allows Salvadorans to apply for cancellation of removal (this is a form of individual amnesty for long-term illegal aliens whose deportation would cause "extreme hardship") under the more-lenient, pre-1996 rules. . . .

The near certainty that temporarily protected Salvadorans will end up staying permanently underlines the fallacy of such humanitarian deferrals of deportation. Nor has the creation of the formal process of TPS made any difference in this regard. . . .

Concerns about temporarily protected aliens settling permanently may be of less concern when relatively small numbers of people are involved, as has been the case with many grants of TPS (see Table 2). But such concerns are salient when large numbers are granted TPS; this is certainly the case with the December 1998 grant of TPS for 18 months to an estimated 90,000 Hondurans and 60,000 Nicaraguans, in response to the devastation wreaked on those countries by Hurricane Mitch. (Advocacy groups were unsuccessful in getting TPS extended to about 500,000 Salvadorans and Guatemalans, though deportations of these groups were suspended for several months.)

The fallout from Hurricane Mitch in Central America is precisely the kind of natural disaster TPS was intended to address, and if the 90,000 Hondurans were to leave after the expiration of their TPS status, then the legislation would have served its purpose (the Nicaraguans won't be leaving because they are already eligible for amnesty under NACARA). But history gives us little reason to expect this will happen; their TPS status is likely to be extended, perhaps replaced by DED, until such time as the aliens in question have either become permanent residents through some other means or until Congress passes legislation legalizing their status. Few, if any, will ever depart voluntarily or be removed.

Prospect of TPS Attracts Illegals

Temporary protection, whether institutionalized or ad hoc, is not merely a tool of foreign policy or a stratagem to avoid deporting politically popular illegal aliens. In recent months it has become clear that the prospect of receiving TPS is also a *magne*t for new illegal immigration. Since the beginning of 1999, thousands of people from Colombia are believed to have arrived illegally or overstayed tourist visas because of that country's deteriorating economy and escalating violence. The Colombian government estimates that 65,000 people left the country in the first four months of 1999, many going to the United States, and that up to 300,000 more could leave by the end of the year. A Colombian ethnic organization in Miami estimates that 15,000 families have fled to South Florida in the past few months, many arriving as tourists but overstaying their visas.

Table 2. Grants of TPS
(with estimates of number of people covered at time of grant)

Bosnia-Herzogovina	400
Burundi	400
El Salvador	190,000
Guinea-Bissau	300
Honduras	90,000
Kosovo	5,000
Kuwait	10,000
Lebanon	27,000
Liberia	8,000
Montserrat	300
Nicaragua	60,000
Rwanda	200
Sierra Leone	4,000
Somalia	2,000
Sudan	4,000

Federal Register, INS

The lobbying effort to procure TPS for these illegal aliens is gaining momentum. In July 1999, thousands of people demonstrated in Miami, Chicago, Houston, and elsewhere, demanding TPS. Rep. Lincoln Diaz-Balart, a Republican congressman from Miami with many Colombian constituents, has written President Clinton demanding looser requirements for granting political asylum to Colombians. And the U.S. Committee for Refugees has started a letter-writing effort to have Colombian illegal aliens granted TPS.

The rhetoric of temporary protection may have a certain

political appeal, and the formal articulation of a TPS mechanism is at least tidier than the extra-legal methods employed before 1990. But it is clear that the concept of temporary protection has not been, and cannot be, successful i.e., truly temporary. It is simply a lie if used as a fig leaf to cover political unwillingness to enforce the law or as a back door to permanent immigration. Therefore, if Congress or the Administration consider it advisable to admit refugees or give amnesty to illegal aliens, simple honesty demands that these actions be called by their real names.

"While . . . [temporary protected status for refugees] might forestall deportation, . . . any advantage would be short-lived and thus hardly an incentive to illegal immigration."

U.S. Refugee Policies Do Not Encourage Illegal Immigration

American Immigration Law Foundation

Some immigration policy critics have claimed that foreigners are taking advantage of American refugee policies by immigrating to the United States illegally. In the following viewpoint, taken from a policy paper produced by the American Immigration Law Foundation (AILF), U.S. refugee policies are defended as a humane and decent response to people fleeing political unrest or other similar conditions in their home countries. Policies such as the granting of "temporary protected status" (TPS) do not worsen the problem of illegal immigration, the authors assert, since many refugees that come to America fully intend to return home. AILF is a nonprofit educational and service organization that works to promote public understanding of immigration law and policy.

As you read, consider the following questions:
1. What conditions are necessary for the granting of TPS status, according to AILF?
2. What is the difference between refugee and asylum status, according to the authors?
3. How do refugees differ from traditional immigrants, as argued by AILF?

Critics have argued that the protection granted to Kosovar Albanians and others fleeing political unrest or natural disasters is "perverse" and serves as a "magnet for new illegal immigration." To their credit, the American people take a much more humanitarian view, including the better than two-to-one majority who say America was right to accept refugees from Kosovo.

Temporary Protected Status

Foreign visitors, students, and businesspeople enter the United States regularly for short periods of time. They are generally issued visas by an American embassy or consulate in their home countries, and then admitted to the United States for a specific period of time by the Immigration and Naturalization Service.

Unfortunately, conditions beyond those visitors' control might prevent their safe return to their home countries. A grandmother from Turkey, visiting her grandchildren in Montana, might find it impossible to return to her homeland immediately after the recent devastating earthquake that occurred while she was away. An exchange student from Kosovo, studying at a college in Oklahoma, might find it impossible to return to his homeland immediately after the Serbian invasion that occurred while he was away. A businessman from Nicaragua, negotiating a global agribusiness contract with a firm in North Carolina, might find it impossible to immediately return to his homeland after Hurricane Mitch devastated Central America last fall.

U.S. immigration law and foreign policy acknowledge these situations and provide foreign visitors to the U.S. with "temporary protected status" (TPS). Congress gave the U.S. Attorney General the authority to designate visitors from a foreign country as eligible for TPS. One of three conditions are necessary. First, TPS may be granted if there is an armed conflict in the visitor's homeland that could cause a serious threat to his safety. Second, TPS may be granted if there is a natural disaster (such as earthquake, flood, drought, etc.) in the visitor's homeland and the visitor's home government is unable to handle the return of visitors. Finally, TPS may be granted if the Attorney General finds extraordinary and temporary conditions in the foreign state that prevent a visitor's safe return.

Generally, an alien applies for TPS if his authorized stay in the U.S. is about to expire. While there is no statistical information from INS to quantify it, theoretically an illegal alien from a TPS-designated country could also apply for the program; while it might forestall deportation or removal from the United States temporarily, any advantage would be short-lived and thus hardly an incentive to illegal immigration.

Other Types of Protection

TPS is by definition a temporary status. Generally, it is granted in one year intervals, with extensions considered annually. However, it presumes the alien will eventually be able to return to his homeland. When that is not possible, the option of applying for refugee or asylum status may be available.

Both statuses are very similar, allowing an alien who is fleeing religious, ethnic, or political persecution to seek safe haven in the United States. The difference between the terms is that asylum is what an alien seeks when he is already in the United States (e.g., the dramatic request shown in the media of a foreign diplomat or athlete seeking asylum), while refugee status applies to someone who has not yet entered the United States (e.g., individuals fleeing a war in Vietnam or Africa).

Each year the United States sets annual ceilings, or limits, on how many asylees and refugees it will accept. For FY2000, the number proposed by the White House is 80,000, with a special provision for an additional 10,000 from Kosovo.

However, just because a certain number are authorized does not mean those refugees will settle permanently in the United States. The plight of Kosovar refugees illustrates this well.

They Want to Go Home

The State Department brought 10,513 Kosovar refugees to America during the recent ethnic cleansing atrocities by Serbian forces. But now that the conflict has ended and NATO peacekeepers have begun to restore safety, the International

FY2000 Proposed Refugee Admissions

Africa	18,000
East Asia	8,000
Europe	47,000
Latin America/Caribbean	3,000
Near East/South Asia	8,000
Unallocated	6,000

American Immigration Law Foundation

Organization for Migration estimates that more than a third of the refugees already want to return to Kosovo. As conditions in Kosovo improve, it is likely many more refugees will return.

Here's what some Kosovars in the U.S. are saying about their refugee status:

"The conditions that I live in here [in the U.S.] are much better than what I'll find back home," said one refugee. "But simply, I love Kosovo more than anything else and more than any other country."

"We just want to go back," said another Kosovar refugee.

"I have to go [home to Kosovo]; my husband is there, and my people," said yet another.

TPS Is a Beacon, Not a Magnet

America's history is founded on providing a safe haven to persecuted and disadvantaged people throughout the world. America has welcomed those fleeing religious persecution beginning with the Pilgrims in the 1600s through Soviet Jews in the 1980s. America has welcomed those fleeing political persecution beginning with the British colonists in the 17th and 18th centuries through Cubans in the 1950s fleeing Castro's communism in Cuba. America has welcomed those fleeing economic and natural disaster including the 19th century Irish fleeing famine through Central Americans fleeing the devastation of Hurricane Mitch just last year.

The protection that America offers, unfortunately often checked by strict numerical limits, shines as a beacon through the misery and suffering of peoples throughout the globe. Unlike traditional immigration, refugees don't seek out America feeling drawn to some magnet; rather they are drawn to the hope and protection we can offer in their direst times of need and despair.

Human decency demands that America open its arms to those in desperate need, with the knowledge that our moral and ethical compasses are guiding us to do the right thing.

Periodical Bibliography

The following articles have been selected to supplement the diverse views presented in this chapter. Addresses are provided for periodicals not indexed in the *Readers' Guide to Periodical Literature*, the *Alternative Press Index*, the *Social Sciences Index*, or the *Index to Legal Periodicals and Books*.

Ken Ellingwood	"Unequal Success in the Quest for Asylum," *Los Angeles Times*, September 28, 2000.
Shirley M. Hufstedler	"Steps to a Better Refugee Policy," *Christian Science Monitor*, June 4, 1997.
Samuel Huntington	"The Special Case of Mexican Immigration," *American Enterprise*, December 2000.
Arthur Jones	"Immigrants Draw Harsh Terms for Simple Mistakes," *National Catholic Reporter*, September 29, 2000.
Brian Jordan	"The Long Arm of Immigration Reform," *Christian Century*, March 18, 1998.
Donald Kerwin	"Looking for Asylum, Suffering in Detention," *Human Rights*, Winter 2001.
Karen Musalo	"Expedited Removal," *Human Rights*, Winter 2001.
Haya El Nasser	"Immigration Advocates Brace for Law's Fallout; Illegals Who Leave USA to Get Visa May Be Barred from Returning for Up to Ten Years," *USA Today*, April 2, 1997.
Kelly Patricia O'Meara	"Breaking the Law Makes You Legal," *Insight*, November 29, 1999.
James S. Robb	"Asylum Ad Absurdum," *Social Contract*, Summer 1997.
Michael Satchell	"A Woman's Right to Stay," *U.S. News & World Report*, January 29, 2001.
Mark Scousen	"Freedom for Everyone...Except the Immigrant," *Freeman*, September 1995.
Julian L. Simon et al.	"Why Control the Borders?" *National Review*, February 1, 1993.
Margaret D. Stock	"Equal Justice for Noncitizens," *Trial*, July 1999.

For Further Discussion

Chapter 1

1. What examples of the harms of illegal immigration does Ted Hayes provide? What specific refutations of these harms does Richard Rayner make, if any? Explain.

2. Unlike Ted Hayes, Richard Rayner provides personal details on the lives and circumstances of individuals who happen to be illegal immigrants. What do you think is the purpose of such personalization? Do you believe it was effective in supporting his arguments? Explain your answers.

3. Does the fact that Richard Rayner is himself an immigrant instead of a native-born American lend more or less validity to his views, in your opinion? Or is it irrelevant to the debate? Why or why not?

4. FAIR argues that poor working Americans are overlooked in the immigration debate. Can this criticism be extended to Robert Scheer's article? Explain.

5. Who do you believe presents the strongest arguments about the effects of illegal immigration on border areas, Glynn Custred or Maria Jiménez? Do you think your views on immigration would be affected if you lived in the areas described by the authors? Why or why not?

6. After reading the viewpoints of Josh Moenning and Mark Krikorian, as well as the others in this chapter, do you believe the problems illegal immigration may cause are the same as those caused by legal immigration? What is the main difference, if any, between the two? Explain.

Chapter 2

1. After reading the viewpoints of Ann Carr and Joseph A. D'Agostino, rank how important you believe family unity should be in formulating immigration policy? Should the fact that many illegal immigrants have family members in the United States weigh heavily in enforcing immigration laws? Why or why not?

2. Should responsibility for the deaths of Mexicans attempting to enter the United States be placed on Mexico, as Samuel Francis contends, or on the United States, as Joseph Nevins argues? Is this an area in which blame could be shared? How much re-

sponsibility should be placed on the immigrants themselves? Explain your answers.

3. On what points, if any, do Jane Slaughter and Wendy McElroy agree on as to the plight of illegal immigrant workers? What are their main differences? Explain.

Chapter 3

1. Michael Scott refers to a "ticking time bomb" and "hordes of illegal aliens" in describing America's illegal immigration situation. Does such language, in your opinion, appeal more to a person's reason or to emotions? Can you find other examples of possibly inflammatory language in the viewpoints of Michael Scott and Saskia Sassen? Explain.

2. What accusation does Miguel Perez make against Republican opponents of amnesty for illegal immigrants? Do such accusations strengthen or weaken his arguments, in your view? Can you find evidence for Perez's assertion in the viewpoints of Michael Scott, Don Feder, or other viewpoints in the chapter? Why or why not?

3. Don Feder talks of "illegal aliens" and mocks the term "undocumented workers." What differences exist between these two terms in meaning? Explain.

4. What does Tom Andres believe to be the message the United States is sending by granting birthright citizenship to children of illegal immigrants? Does Jack Kemp address this issue in his article? Who do you believe presents a stronger case for or against birthright citizenship? Explain your answers.

5. Both Larry Craig and Howard L. Berman agree that the status quo with regards to immigrant farm workers is unacceptable. What do they find objectionable? Can you summarize the main areas in which they disagree? Explain.

Chapter 4

1. FAIR argues that the benefits of Section 110 outweigh its costs, while Bronwyn Lance argues that its costs exceed the benefits. What costs and benefits of the legislation do both authors describe? Which do you think are most important?

2. Which of Kevin R. Johnson and Robert J. Samuelson's arguments revolve around economic concerns? Which do not? Does one author emphasize economic matters more than the other? Do you believe economic interests should be the fundamental concern of immigration policy? Explain.

3. Mark Krikorian argues that there is a large gap between theory and reality over how "temporary protected status" is given to refugees, and suggests that the debate over refugee policy is dishonest because it ignores this fact? Could this criticism be applied to the viewpoint of the American Immigration Law Foundation, in your view? Defend your answer.

Organizations to Contact

The editors have compiled the following list of organizations concerned with the issues debated in this book. The descriptions are derived from materials provided by the organizations. All have publications or information available for interested readers. This list was compiled on the date of publication of the present volume; the information provided here may change. Be aware that many organizations take several weeks or longer to respond to inquiries, so allow as much time as possible.

American Civil Liberties Union (ACLU)
132 W. 43d St., New York, NY 10036
(212) 944-9800 • fax: (212) 921-7916
website: www.aclu.org

The ACLU is a national organization that champions the rights found in the Declaration of Independence and the U.S. Constitution. The ACLU Immigrants' Rights Project works with refugees and immigrants facing deportation, and with immigrants in the workplace. It has published reports, position papers, and a book, *The Rights of Aliens and Refugees*, that detail what freedoms immigrants and refugees have under the U.S. Constitution.

American Friends Service Committee (AFSC)
1501 Cherry St., Philadelphia, PA 19102
(215) 241-7000 • fax: (215) 241-7275
e-mail: afscinfo@afsc.org • website: www.afsc.org

The AFSC is a Quaker organization that attempts to relieve human suffering and find new approaches to world peace and social justice through nonviolence. It lobbies against what it believes to be unfair immigration laws, especially sanctions criminalizing the employment of illegal immigrants. It has published *Sealing Our Borders: The Human Toll*, a report documenting human rights violations committed by law enforcement agents against immigrants.

American Immigration Control Foundation (AICF)
PO Box 525, Monterey, VA 24465
(703) 468-2022 • fax: (703) 468-2024

AICF is an independent research and education organization that believes massive immigration, especially illegal immigration, is harming America. It calls for an end to illegal immigration and for stricter controls on legal immigration. The foundation publishes the monthly newsletter *Border Watch* and two pamphlets: John Vinson's *Immigration Out of Control*, and Lawrence Auster's *The Path to National Suicide: An Essay on Immigration and Multiculturalism.*

American Immigration Lawyers Association (AILA)
1400 I St. NW, Suite 1200, Washington, DC 20005
(202) 216-2400 • fax: (202) 371-9449
website: www.aila.org

AILA is a professional association of lawyers who work in the field of immigration and nationality law. It publishes the *AILA Immigration Journal* and compiles and distributes a continuously updated bibliography of government and private documents on immigration laws and regulations.

Americans for Immigration Control (AIC)
725 Second St. NE, Suite 307, Washington, DC 20002
(202) 543-3719 • fax: (202) 543-5811

AIC is a lobbying organization that works to influence Congress to adopt legal reforms that would reduce U.S. immigration. It calls for increased funding for the U.S. Border Patrol and the deployment of military forces to prevent illegal immigration. It also supports sanctions against employers who hire illegal immigrants and opposes amnesty for such immigrants. AIC offers articles and brochures which state its position on immigration.

Americas Watch (AW)
485 Fifth Ave., New York, NY 10017
(212) 972-8400 • fax: (212) 972-0905

AW, a division of Human Rights Watch, is an organization that promotes human rights, especially for Latin Americans. It publicizes human rights violations and encourages international protests against governments responsible for them. AW has published *Brutality Unchecked: Human Rights Abuses Along the U.S. Border with Mexico.*

The Brookings Institution
1775 Massachusetts Ave. NW, Washington, DC 20036-2188
(202) 797-6104 • fax: (202) 797-6319
e-mail: brookinfo@brook.edu • website: www.brook.edu

The institution, founded in 1927, is a liberal research and education organization that publishes material on economics, government, and foreign policy. It publishes analyses of immigration issues in its quarterly journal, *Brookings Review*, and in various books and reports.

California Coalition for Immigration Reform (CCIR)
PO Box 2744-117, Huntington Beach, CA 92649
(714) 665-2500 • fax: (714) 846-9682
website: www.ccir.net

CCIR is a grassroots volunteer organization representing Americans concerned with illegal immigration. It seeks to educate and inform the public and to effectively ensure enforcement of the nation's immigration laws. CCIR publishes alerts, bulletins, and the monthly newsletter *911*.

Cato Institute
1000 Massachusetts Ave. NW, Washington, DC 20001-5403
(202) 842-0200 • fax: (202) 842-3490
website: www.cato.org

The institute is a libertarian public policy research foundation dedicated to stimulating policy debate. It believes immigration is good for the U.S. economy and favors easing immigration restrictions. As well as various articles on immigration, the institute has published Julian L. Simon's book *The Economic Consequences of Immigration*.

Center for Immigrants Rights (CIR)
48 St. Mark's Pl., 4th Fl, New York, NY 10003
(212) 505-6890

The center offers immigrants information concerning their rights. It provides legal support, advocacy, and assistance to immigrants and strives to influence immigration policy. The center publishes fact sheets on immigrant rights and immigration law and the quarterly newsletter *CIR Report*.

Center for Immigration Studies
1522 K St., NW, Suite 820, Washington, DC 20005-1202
(202) 466-8185 • fax: (202) 466-8076
e-mail: center@cis.org • website: www.cis.org

The center studies the effects of immigration on the economic, social, demographic, and environmental conditions in the United States. It believes that the large number of recent immigrants has become a burden on America and favors reforming immigration laws to make them consistent with U.S. interests. The center publishes reports, position papers, and the quarterly journal *Scope*.

El Rescate
2675 W. Olympic Blvd., Los Angeles, CA 90006
(213) 387-3284

El Rescate provides free legal and social services to Central American refugees. It is involved in federal litigation to uphold the constitutional rights of refugees and illegal immigrants. It compiles and distributes articles and information and publishes the newsletter *El Rescate*.

Federation for American Immigration Reform (FAIR)

1666 Connecticut Ave. NW, Suite 400, Washington, DC 20009
(202) 328-7004 • fax: (202) 387-3447
e-mail: info@fairus.org • website: www.fairus.org

FAIR works to stop illegal immigration and to limit legal immigration. It believes that the growing flood of immigrants into the United States causes higher unemployment and taxes social services. FAIR has published many reports and position papers, including *Ten Steps to Securing America's Borders* and *Immigration 2000: The Century of the New American Sweatshop*.

Foundation for Economic Education, Inc. (FEE)

30 S. Broadway, Irvington, NY 10533
(914) 591-7230 • fax: (914) 591-8910
e-mail: fee@fee.org • website: www.fee.org

FEE publishes information and research in support of capitalism, free trade, and limited government. It occasionally publishes articles opposing government restrictions on immigration in its monthly magazine, the *Freeman*.

The Heritage Foundation

214 Massachusetts Ave. NE, Washington, DC 20002-4999
(202) 546-4400 • fax: (202) 546-8328
e-mail: info@heritage.org • website: www.heritage.org

The foundation is a conservative public policy research institute. It has published articles pertaining to immigration in its Backgrounder series and in its quarterly journal, *Policy Review*.

National Alliance Against Racist and Political Repression (NAARPR)

11 John St., Rm. 702, New York, NY 10038
(212) 406-3330 • fax: (212) 406-3542

NAARPR is a coalition of political, labor, church, civic, student, and community organizations that oppose the many forms of human rights repression in the United States. It seeks to end the harassment and deportation of illegal immigrant workers. The alliance publishes pamphlets and a quarterly newsletter, *The Organizer*.

National Coalition of Advocates for Students (NCAS)
100 Boylston St., Suite 737, Boston, MA 02116-4610
(617) 357-8507• fax: (617) 357-9549
e-mail: ncasmfe@mindspring.com • website: www.ncas1.org
NCAS is a national network of child advocacy organizations that work on public school issues. Through its Immigrant Student Program it works to ensure that immigrants are given sufficient and appropriate education. The coalition has published two book-length reports: *New Voices: Immigrant Students in U.S. Public Schools* and *Immigrant Students: Their Legal Right of Access to Public Schools.*

National Council of La Raza (NCLR)
1111 19th St. NW, Suite 1000, Washington, DC 20036
(202) 289-1380 • fax: (202) 289-8173
website: www.nclr.org
NCLR is a national organization that seeks to improve opportunities for Americans of Hispanic descent. It conducts research on many issues, including immigration, and opposes restrictive immigration laws. The council publishes and distributes congressional testimony and reports, including *Unfinished Business: The Immigration Control and Reform Act of 1986* and *Unlocking the Golden Door: Hispanics and the Citizenship Process.*

National Immigration Forum
220 I St. NE, Suite 220, Washington, DC 20002-4362
(202) 544-0004 • fax: (202) 544-1905
website: www.immigrationforum.org
The forum believes that legal immigrants strengthen America and that welfare benefits do not attract illegal immigrants. It supports effective measures aimed at curbing illegal immigration and promotes programs and policies that help refugees and immigrants assimilate into American society. The forum publishes the quarterly newsletter the *Golden Door* and the bimonthly newsletter *Immigration Policy Matters.*

The National Network for Immigrant and Refugee Rights
310 Eighth St., Suite 307, Oakland, CA 94607
(510) 465-1984 • fax: (510) 465-1885
website: www.nnirr.org/frame.html
The network includes community, church, labor, and legal groups committed to the cause of equal rights for all immigrants. These groups work to end discrimination and unfair treatment of illegal immigrants and refugees. The network aims to strengthen and co-

ordinate educational efforts among immigration advocates nation-wide. It publishes a monthly newsletter, *Network News*.

Negative Population Growth, Inc. (NPG)

1717 Massachusetts Ave., NW, Suite 101, Washington, DC 20036
(202) 667-8950 • fax: (202) 667-8953
e-mail: npg@npg.org • website: www.npg.org

NPG believes that world population must be reduced and that the United States is already overpopulated. It calls for an end to illegal immigration and an annual cap on legal immigration of 200,000 people. This would achieve "zero net migration" because 200,000 people exit the country each year, according to NPG. NPG frequently publishes position papers on population and immigration in its *NPG Forum*.

The Rockford Institute

928 N. Main St., Rockford, IL 61103-7061
(815) 964-5053 • fax: (815) 965-1827
e-mail: info@rockfordinsitute.org
website: www.rockfordinstitute.org

The institute is a conservative research center that studies capitalism, religion, and liberty. It has published numerous articles questioning immigration and legalization policies in its monthly magazine, *Chronicles*.

United States Immigration and Naturalization Service (INS)

425 I St. NW, Room 4236, Washington, DC 20536
(202) 514-4316
website: www.ins.usdoj.gov

The INS, an agency of the Department of Justice, is charged with enforcing immigration laws and regulations, as well as administering immigrant-related services including the granting of asylum and refugee status. It produces numerous reports and evaluations on selected programs. Statistics and information on immigration and immigration laws as well as congressional testimony, fact sheets, and other materials are available on its website.

U.S. Border Control (USBC)

8180 Greensboro Dr., Suite 1070, McLean, VA 22102
(703) 356-6568 • fax: (202) 478-0254
e-mail: info@usbc.org • website: www.usbc.org

USBC is a lobbying group dedicated to ending illegal immigration by reforming U.S. immigration policies and securing American borders. It publishes articles on U.S. border and immigration policies in its newsletter, *Border Alert*, and on its website.

Bibliography of Books

Brent Ashabranner — *Our Beckoning Borders: Illegal Immigration to America.* New York: Cobblehill Books, 1996.

Roy Beck — *The Case Against Immigration.* New York: W.W. Norton, 1996.

George J. Borjas — *Heaven's Door: Immigration Policy and the American Economy.* Princeton, NJ: Princeton University Press, 1999.

Peter Brimelow — *Alien Nation: Common Sense About America's Immigration Disaster.* New York: Random House, 1995.

Leo R. Chavez — *Shadowed Lives: Undocumented Immigrants in American Society.* Fort Worth, TX: Harcourt Brace College Publishers, 1997.

Gabriel J. Chin and Morgan Sprague, eds. — *The United States Commission on Immigration Reform: The Interim and Final Reports and Commentary.* Buffalo, NY: William S. Hein & Co., 1999.

Ko-lin Chin — *Smuggled Chinese: Clandestine Immigration to the United States.* Philadelphia: Temple University Press, 1999.

Wayne A. Cornelius, Philip L. Martin, and James F. Hollifield — *Controlling Immigration: A Global Perspective.* Stanford, CA: Stanford University Press, 1994.

Roger Daniels and Otis L. Graham — *Debating American Immigration, 1882–Present.* Lanham, MD: Roman & Littlefield, 2001.

Venson C. Davis — *Blood on the Border: Criminal Behavior and Illegal Immigration Along the Southern U.S. Border.* New York: Vantage Press, 1993.

Debra L. Delaet — *U.S. Immigration Policy in an Age of Rights.* Westport, CT: Praeger, 2000.

Richard M. Ebeling and Jacob G. Hornberger, eds. — *The Case for Free Trade and Open Immigration.* Fairfax, VA: Future of Freedom Foundation, 1995.

Georgie Anne Geyer — *Americans No More.* New York: Atlantic Monthly Press, 1996.

David W. Haines and Karen Elaine Rosenblum, eds. — *Illegal Immigration in America: A Reference Handbook.* Westport, CT: Greenwood Press, 1999.

Nigel Harris — *The New Untouchables: Immigration and the New World Worker.* New York: St. Martin's Press, 1995.

William Hawkins   *Importing Revolution: Open Borders and the Radical Agenda*. Monterey, VA: American Immigration Control Foundation, 1995.

Helene Hayes   *U.S. Immigration Policy and the Undocumented: Ambivalent Laws, Furtive Lies*. Westport, CT: Praeger, 2001.

John Isbister   *The Immigration Debate: Remaking America*. West Hartford, CT: Kumarian Press, 1996.

Peter Kwong   *Forbidden Workers: Illegal Chinese Immigrants and American Labor*. New York: New Press, 1998.

David Kyle and   *Global Human Smuggling: Comparative Perspectives*. Baltimore, MD: Johns Hopkins University Press, 2001.
Rey Koslowski, eds.

Gerald Leinwand   *American Immigration: Should the Open Door Be Closed?* New York: Franklin Watts, 1995.

Joel Millman   *The New Americans: How Immigrants Renew Our Country, Our Economy, and Our Values*. New York: Viking, 1997.

Juan F. Perea, ed.   *Immigrants Out! The New Nativism and the Anti-Immigrant Impulse in the United States*. New York: New York University Press, 1997.

Mei Ling Rein et al.,   *Immigration and Illegal Aliens: Burden or Blessing?* Wylie, TX: Information Plus, 1999.
eds.

Sebastian Rotella   *Twilight on the Line: Underworlds and Politics at the U.S.-Mexico Border*. New York: W.W. Norton, 1998.

Peter H. Shuck   *Citizens, Strangers, and In-Betweens: Essays on Immigration and Citizenship*. Boulder, CO: Westview Press, 1998.

Phil Williams, ed.   *Illegal Immigration and Commercial Sex: The New Slave Trade*. New York: Frank & Cass, 1999.

Chisato Yoshida   *Illegal Immigration and Economic Welfare*. Heidelberg, Germany: Physica Verlag, 2000.

Index

fraudulent collection of, by illegal
    immigrants, 19
unions, 98, 101, 121, 144
    difficulty of organizing, for
        immigrant workers, 88, 95, 99, 100
    immigrant workers' need for, 90–94,
        102
    see also AFL-CIO; *names of individual
        unions*
UNITE (Union of Needletrades,
    Industrial and Textile Employees),
    98, 101
United Farm Workers, 101, 144
United States, 13
    economy of, can absorb many
        immigrants, 36–37
    and efforts to discourage immigrants
        from dangerous border crossings,
        85
    identity of, 29
    as land of immigrants, 38, 59,
        60–61, 169
    illegal immigrants not a threat to, 17,
        22, 30
        con, 170–72
    immigration laws of, 13
    issue of mobility in, 51–52
    Mexico's desire to invade, 84, 86
    and need for agreement with Mexico
        regarding labor migration, 166
    numbers of people wishing to
        immigrate to, 12
    open border policy not politically
        viable in, 165
    shortage of farm workers in, 140
        exaggerated, 143
    threat to sovereignty of, 14, 17, 21
    values of

challenged by immigration debate,
    30
include right to criticize
    government, 114
resistance to police-state measures
    prompted by, 82
see also Mexico, U.S. border with
United Students Against Sweatshops, 96
University of California, 110
University of California, Davis, 163
University of Pennsylvania, 96
Urban Institute, 24, 26, 50, 171
Urban Institute Press, 110
Uriostegua, Jose Luis, 81, 82

Vallone, Peter, 101
Vance, Larry, 46
Vega, Rafael, 12
violence, domestic, 54
visa violations, 149, 150, 154, 155, 164
    deportation for, is rare, 153
    and entry/exit control system, 156,
        157
    impracticality of, 158–62
    INS failure to deal with, 151–52
    need to deal with, 30

Wall Street Journal (newspaper), 170
Washington State, 159
welfare, 108
    and AFDC, 27
Wellman, William, 47
Wilson, Pete, 18, 25, 41, 79
Wissinger, Kent, 77
Worker Rights Consortium, 96
World Bank, 169
World Trade Organization, 119
Wortman, Julie A., 69